EXCEPTIONALITY, *12*(4), 193–194
Copyright © 2004, Taylor & Francis

T0347575

PREFACE

Critical Issues in Training
Special Education Teachers

Teacher training has been a hot topic for the past few years, beginning with President Bush signing into law the No Child Left Behind (NCLB) Act in January 2002 (Public Law 107–110; http://www.ed.gov/policy/elsec/leg/esea02/index.html). Because of the serious consequences associated with the NCLB Act, many policy discussions have focused on the barriers to implementation and the difficulties states have putting together the required pieces related to standards assessments and teacher quality (Laitsch, 2003). Although many areas in education are experiencing quality teacher shortages, the shortages of teachers qualified in the area of special education are of critical concern. Recently, this shortage has received attention from policymakers at the national level as well as state-level officials and faculty within teacher training institutions. Many state-level officials are aware of the difficulties inherent in ensuring that all special education teachers are highly qualified. Many teacher training programs are being asked to demonstrate how their candidates impact children's achievement.

In response to these shortages and the recent federal mandates, alternatives to traditional teacher preparation are proliferating. Will these alternatives be more failed attempts to increase the quality of teachers? The articles in this issue of *Exceptionality* discuss a number of the issues relevant to special education teacher training: the meaning of highly qualified teachers, especially in the area of special education; the comparison of traditionally and alternatively trained special education teachers; and the reflections of alternatively trained first-year special educators. In addition, this issue provides a reflection of the past 20 years of preparing special education teachers.

Leading off this special issue on teacher training issues in special education, Gelman, Pullen, and Kauffman address the meaning of highly qualified as suggested in the reauthorization of the Elementary and Secondary Education Act (NCLB; Public Law 107–110; http://www.ed.gov/policy/elsec/leg/esea02/index.html). Gelman et al. question the definitions, goals, and steps to accomplishment of the Act. They also provide a road map of specific goals to accomplish high-quality professional development. Kauffman (1993) suggested that only a realistic, long-term commitment and investment will result in better teachers, professional development, and student achievement. There is no quick fix that will lead to greater student achievement.

In the next article, Sindelar, Daunic, and Rennells present findings from a comparative study of three teacher preparation programs: traditional, university–district partnership, and district add-on. The notion that all alternative programs are not alike has stirred the demand for more research in which program variants are compared. The graduates were observed during their first year of teaching using the Praxis III assessment. A larger sample completed a follow-up questionnaire assessing preparedness and efficacy, and a subset of them had principals submit ratings. The findings are discussed in terms of the distinction between formal and procedural knowledge. The differences are noteworthy.

Next, deBettencourt and Howard describe a federally funded alternative licensure program. The program participants were surveyed during their first year of teaching. Their reflections on the training program, their school-district mentors, and their teaching experiences are discussed. The authors conclude that it is critical that research begin to document the components of successful alternative licensure programs.

The final article by Bauer, Johnson, and Sapona discusses the dramatic changes in the preparation of special educators since the Individuals with Disabilities Education Act (Public Law 105–71; http://www.ed.gov/offices/OSERS/Policy/IDEA/the_law.html) was implemented. Special education teachers must deal with changes in the political contexts in which they work as well as changes in the youth and families with whom they work. As a consequence of those changes, how we prepare teachers has become much more complex. Teacher education programs are being asked to demonstrate how their candidates impact children's achievement in ways that we have never had to before. Although we face increased accountability, we have additional tools, such as the use of performance assessments and technology, as well as innovative research strategies to determine the impact of our teaching candidates on children's learning.

The articles in this special issue serve as additional voices on teacher training in special education—an important topic in need of continued discourse.

REFERENCES

Elementary and Secondary Education Act. (2001). *No Child Left Behind Act of 2001*. Washington, DC: U.S. Department of Education. Retrieved November 23, 2004, from http://www.ed.gov/policy/elsec/leg/esea02/index.html

Individuals with Disabilities Education Act. (1997). *The Individuals with Disabilities Education Act Amendments of 1997*. Retrieved November 23, 2004, from http://www.cec.sped.org/law_res/doc/law/download Law.php

Kauffman, J. M. (1993). How we might achieve the radical reform of special education. *Exceptional Children, 60*, 6–16.

Laitsch, D. (2003, October). Reflections on implementation: Two years and counting. *Infobrief, 35*, 1–8.

Laurie U. deBettencourt
Guest Editor

EXCEPTIONALITY, *12*(4), 195–207

ARTICLES

The Meaning of Highly Qualified
and a Clear Road Map to Accomplishment

Jennifer A. Gelman, Patricia L. Pullen, and James M. Kauffman
Curriculum, Instruction, and Special Education
University of Virginia

The reauthorization of the Elementary and Secondary Education (No Child Left Behind) Act is questioned with reference to the requirement that every state ensure that all special education teachers are highly qualified and are receiving high-quality professional development. The conclusion is that the act lacks clear definitions, realistic goals, and clear steps to accomplishment. A road map of specific steps and appropriate definitions and goals are recommended.

On January 8, 2002, the reauthorization of the Elementary and Secondary Education Act (ESEA), also called the No Child Left Behind (NCLB) Act, was signed into law. The bill covers many aspects of education policy, but one area of particular interest to the special education community is the requirement that every state ensure that all special education teachers are highly qualified and are receiving high-quality professional development (ESEA, 2001, Section 1119). These are worthy goals, and reaching them has been attempted for decades. Unfortunately, we have never been able to attain them. Now, with the implementation of NCLB, these goals are supposed to become realities (Cochran-Smith, 2002; U.S. Department of Education & Office of Postsecondary Education, 2003).

NCLB offers a definition of highly qualified, and steps are highlighted to implement high-quality professional development. However, the definition and the steps are far from clear and specific. In fact, as others have pointed out, the NCLB requirements appear to be narrow, inadequate, and based primarily on pretense (Berry, Hoke, & Hirsch, 2004; Rebell & Hunter, 2004). Furthermore, the demands of NCLB do not focus on systemic reform but defer to state ideas of what constitutes highly qualified (Brownell,

---

Requests for reprints should be sent to Jennifer A. Gelman, 199 North View Circle, Warrenton, VA 20186. E-mail: jag4g@virginia.edu

Hirsch, & Seo, 2004). Part of the problem is that although NCLB purports to set standards for students and teachers, the standards are really up to the 50 states.

Without clear and specific definitions and steps, it is impossible to achieve any goal, worthy as it may be. We outline what we believe should be the definition of a highly qualified special educator. In addition, we offer a road map of specific steps to accomplish high-quality professional development.

THE HISTORY OF FAILED ATTEMPTS

The message from NCLB is not a new one. For decades, the United States has worked to improve public schools. Dozens of reports on public education have described the poor quality of public schools, and much of the blame has been placed on teachers and teacher educators. Yet, are teachers and teacher educators the ones to blame? Have past attempts given teachers and teacher educators the tools to improve the quality of public schools? History shows that efforts designed to produce better outcomes for public education have lacked long-term commitment, dedicated follow through, specific steps to achieve goals, and appropriate resources (Futrell, 2000). Moreover, teaching and the education of teachers have not been based on reliable evidence about what works and what does not (Hirsch, 1996).

In 1968, the National Institute for Advanced Study in Teaching Disadvantaged Youth published *Teachers for the Real World* (B. O. Smith, 1969), which proposed the development of different teacher preparation. The goal was for public schools, universities, and communities to work together to provide more effective teacher preparation. The report generated discussion, but no specific steps for implementation followed (Futrell, 2000). Its fate was similar to that of previous attempts to reform teacher education (Goodlad, 1990).

In 1980, the National Teacher Corps proposed an outline for reforming teacher education, including a complete change in the program of professional preparation (B. O. Smith, Silverman, Borg, & Fry, 1980). Yet, only a small number of universities became involved in this educational reform. The lack of university commitment to teacher education led to failure (Futrell, 2000).

The National Commission on Excellence in Education made an attempt in 1983 to improve education with its report entitled *A Nation at Risk*. This report called for a commitment of support and resources to education. Although the goals were appropriate, the lack of follow through made them impossible to achieve (Goodlad, 1990).

Head Start, a studied reform, offered promise due to the evidence found from other countries that had implemented early-intervention programs. The Head Start program failed to adopt knowledge-based curricula, though, which were used in these other studied programs. Due to the failure to follow other successful programs with fidelity, the benefits of an additional reform were extremely disappointing (Hirsch, 1996).

The 1990s started with a new educational reform in President George H. W. Bush's State of the Union speech. The first President Bush called for every student to enter school ready to learn. High schools were to increase the graduation rate to 90%, and the United States was to be rated first in the world in math and science. These goals were to be accomplished by the year 2000. However, the lofty goals lacked direction and steps for action. Once again, reform failed to bring education what it desperately needed.

Throughout history many ambitious reforms have been proposed. Despite the various attempts, researchers have found a lack of significant difference in teacher education programs since the 1930s. Surprisingly, the series of disappointments has not led education experts to question why so many attempts to reform are not succeeding. Reluctance and inability to sustain efforts have created failure in spite of good intentions. Without commitment, a realistic plan, and proper resources, the quality of education will remain poor (Futrell, 2000; Goodlad, 1990; Hirsch, 1996).

WHY DO WE KEEP ATTEMPTING
TO ACCOMPLISH THESE GOALS?

With dozens of failed attempts to increase the quality of teachers and professional development, one may question the point of continued efforts to accomplish these goals. Research has shown that highly effective teachers increase student achievement more than ineffective teachers and that teachers' knowledge influences student outcomes. It also suggests that if every classroom had an effective teacher, students would exhibit higher academic achievement (Kaplan & Owings, 2003).

The results of a study examining whether certified teachers affect student performance more than undercertified teachers have clear implications for education reform (Laczko-Kerr & Berliner, 2002). Many teachers are now trained in alternative programs instead of traditional certification programs. Due to the lack of standards in alternative programs, teachers from these programs are entering the field of education with little or no experience in the classroom, poor skills in content areas, and inadequate self-confidence. In short, teachers from alternative certification programs are entering the field undercertified. The data comparing certified and undercertified teachers in reading, math, and language arts indicated that students of undercertified teachers did not perform as well as students of certified teachers (Laczko-Kerr & Berliner, 2002).

A relation between the basic skills of teachers and student achievement has been found. When students have an effective teacher for at least 3 years, achievement scores have increased more than 50 points in math and 35 points in reading (on a 100-point scale) on standardized tests. Students in classrooms with the least effective teachers have shown close to no academic growth. Therefore, consecutive years with effective teachers can increase student outcomes in low-achieving, middle-achieving, and high-achieving students (Kaplan & Owings, 2003).

A teacher's content knowledge has been linked to improved student outcomes. In a study of the effects of teacher's content knowledge, findings revealed that students achieved more when instructed by teachers who had a college major or minor in the subject area in which they taught (Kaplan & Owings, 2003).

In addition, researchers have compared the effects of in-field and out-of-field teaching. In-field teachers have a major or minor in the area of content they are teaching, but out-of-field teachers do not. Studies have indicated that in-field teaching produces greater student achievement than out-of-field teaching. Similar research evidence has been found as well with the comparison of teachers with and without a master's degree.

Students of teachers with a master's degree outperformed students of teachers without a master's degree (Laczko-Kerr & Berliner, 2002).

Although a teacher's content knowledge has been linked to increased student achievement, research has shown that these skills alone will not produce greater gains for students. A successful teacher has a background in effective teaching methods, and these teaching methods cannot be learned on the job (Laczko-Kerr & Berliner, 2002).

In addition to content knowledge, experience has been linked to successful teaching. Fieldwork experiences offered by teacher preparation programs are powerful. Research suggests that fieldwork may be the most valuable force offered by teacher education (Laczko-Kerr & Berliner, 2002).

Another element linked to greater student outcomes is education coursework. One of the strong predictors of teaching effectiveness found by researchers is education coursework (Kaplan & Owings, 2003). Some researchers have found education coursework to be a better predictor than content knowledge (Laczko-Kerr & Berliner, 2002). These findings, along with the findings from many other studies, have revealed the importance of the continuation of attempts to make every teacher highly qualified.

Of course, every finding and every conclusion has its exceptions. True, some teachers poorly prepared by the criteria we have discussed (i.e., a degree in the subject they are teaching, preparation to teach) will be highly successful, and some who have been well prepared by those criteria will fail. However, using outliers (those clearly atypical) to draw conclusions is not an intelligent decision (Kauffman, 2002).

THE AMBIGUOUS NCLB DEFINITION OF HIGHLY QUALIFIED

Due to the research evidence on the effects of high-quality teachers, NCLB has mandated that every teacher be highly qualified by the end of the 2005–2006 school year. The spirit and the intent of the act are easy to agree with, but the definition of highly qualified must be analyzed (U.S. Department of Education & Office of Postsecondary Education, 2003).

There are many elements of the NCLB definition of highly qualified teachers that lack clarity and specificity. One requirement for elementary, middle, and secondary teachers is to "be fully licensed or certified by the state" (Education Commission of the States [ECS], 2003). There is no information on what defines full state certification. Is this different from standard certification? If so, how is it different? Without this information, progress toward this ambiguous requirement cannot be measured (ECS, 2003; see also Rebell & Hunter, 2004).

Another requirement of NCLB is that teachers "not have any certification or licensure requirements waived on an emergency, temporary or provisional basis" (ECS, 2003). What will happen to teachers who do not meet this requirement? Will they be forced to stop teaching? There will be teachers who do not meet this requirement. How will school districts respond to this reality? NCLB does not explain (ECS, 2003).

A third requirement for new and existing teachers is to "have at least a bachelor's degree and pass a state test demonstrating subject knowledge and teaching skills" (ECS, 2003) in all subjects taught. The state test for demonstrating subject knowledge and teaching skills must be rigorous. The meaning of a rigorous state test is not clarified. Traditionally, states have been given the power to determine minimum passing scores. Therefore, each state has different expectations regarding what a teacher should know. Should different states have different requirements for becoming highly qualified? From the description of NCLB requirements needed to be highly qualified, states continue to have the control over determining a passing score. Therefore, each state can have a different interpretation of what score on any test defines highly qualified. In Minnesota, the teacher basic skills test had a 1% failure rate (Laczko-Kerr & Berliner, 2002). Does this represent high qualification of those who pass the Minnesota test? NCLB leaves this decision up to individual states. It does not seem possible for all teachers to be highly qualified with continued variability among states. Once again, NCLB has left this requirement ambiguous (McNergney & Imig, 2003).

For teachers to become highly qualified they may have a credential from an alternative teacher program. Many alternative teacher programs are poorly designed and do not include critical teacher experiences and training. These programs, as well as traditional certification programs, vary considerably. Therefore, it is difficult to understand how teachers from varying certification programs could all be considered highly qualified. NCLB does not address this area of uncertainty (Laczko-Kerr & Berliner, 2002).

The President's Commission on Excellence in Special Education (PCESE, 2002) discussed how teacher preparation programs have failed to provide adequate knowledge and skills to work with all students. The PCESE also reports that teacher preparation faculty lack the necessary knowledge to instruct teachers. If this is true, it is unclear how a teacher can meet the demands of NCLB to be highly qualified when teacher preparation programs are deficient in the essential areas to train highly qualified teachers (PCESE, 2002).

AN APPROPRIATE DEFINITION OF HIGHLY QUALIFIED

For a requirement to be understood and implemented, it must be clear and precise. To give greater value to a requirement, it should be supported by research as well. In addition, a requirement should be standardized across the country to ensure that every teacher reflects that same standard.

NCLB states that every teacher must have full state certification to be highly qualified. The act also states that all teachers must demonstrate competence in their subject areas. An appropriate explanation of full state certification must be provided. In addition, an adequate plan for how teachers are to demonstrate their competence needs to be outlined. A nationwide definition of what full state certification and subject competency are must be known. Or does research show that different locations need varying levels of high qualifications for teachers?

Every school district needs to be striving to meet the same requirements in the same way. States should not have different definitions of and expectations for highly qualified teachers. Children across the country deserve to have access to the most qualified teachers regardless of the state in which they live.

The 2001–2002 teacher licensure requirements for each state varied considerably (Youngs, Odden, & Porter, 2003). Of the 50 states, 37 required teacher candidates to pass a test of basic skills, 33 states assessed new teachers' knowledge of subject matter, 26 states tested pedagogical knowledge, and 9 states assessed classroom performance. Unfortunately, research evidence to support the effectiveness of these state policies on student achievement is scarce. States should only implement teacher candidate requirements that have been proven to increase student outcomes. Once requirements have been proven to be effective, then all states need to implement these requirements in a manner that replicates the effective methods found in research studies.

For every state to be working toward meeting the same requirements in the same way, a detailed description of full national certification must be given. Specific assessments should be used to test teacher proficiency, and standard passing scores should be used for teachers across the country (McNergney & Imig, 2003; U.S. Department of Education & Office of Postsecondary Education, 2003).

Student teaching experience is critical to teacher preparation. Therefore, a full national certification should include an intensive student teaching experience that occurs over an extended period of time. Full national certification should also require that teachers demonstrate strong skills in the content area in which they will teach. This full national certification should ensure that teachers have a thorough understanding of curriculum, student ability, and motivation. Another area in which full national certification must ensure teachers' competence is the way to transform content knowledge into information that is meaningful to students. Therefore, teachers must not only have content knowledge skills, but skills in teaching methods as well. Many certification programs have not trained teachers well in all these areas, and this must not continue (Laczko-Kerr & Berliner, 2002).

States were asked by NCLB to report the number of teachers who did not meet the NCLB demands to be highly qualified. The majority of states claim their teachers are qualified. Thirty-three states have reported that at least 80% of classes in the core subjects have highly qualified teachers. More than half the states reported that schools in high-poverty areas did not have fewer highly qualified teachers than schools in areas without poverty. This information seems questionable when many studies have found schools in high-poverty areas suffer from shortages of qualified teachers (Keller, 2003b). It does not appear that states are taking this opportunity to acknowledge that there is a need for better teachers. Maybe these reports are a result of the ambiguous definition of the NCLB requirements. It is also possible that states have not accepted the changes imposed on them.

It is shocking that states are not demanding more answers regarding the requirements of NCLB. It is hard to understand how Wisconsin reported that 98.6% of its classes have highly qualified teachers when the requirements lack clarity and specific definitions. This is a good demonstration of why states should not be given the authority to define the term highly qualified. It is evident that the current system, in most states, does not produce highly qualified teachers when teacher competency tests have a 99% passing rate and credential programs vary from university to university. This seems to mean that states are content with a low standard for teachers, which is intolerable. Therefore, a nationwide standard must be set for teachers (Keller, 2003b; Laczko-Kerr & Berliner, 2002).

If teachers are expected to be highly qualified, appropriate training programs must be available to assist teachers to meet this goal. The PCESE has reported that preparation programs in special education do not have the necessary skills to produce highly qualified teachers. Demanding that all teachers be highly qualified is nonsensical without all of the proper supports in place. A logical first step would be to focus primarily on improving teacher education programs before placing these requirements on teachers (PCESE, 2002).

CHALLENGES FOR SPECIAL EDUCATION

The demand for qualified special educators is growing into a crisis (Billingsley, 2004). The shortage of qualified special education teachers is so great that any person with a bachelor's degree could be placed in a special education classroom on an emergency credential (Lang & Fox, 2003). Under NCLB, this is not considered acceptable. Although the goal of making every special educator highly qualified is worthy, the barriers to recruiting and retaining these teachers must be lifted (Whitaker, 2003).

Special education teachers face a variety of difficulties that make their challenge virtually impossible. Many are left to teach without a curriculum, materials, support, and experienced special educators with which to collaborate. All of these factors mean that teachers are likely to be far from highly qualified. With all of these challenges, it is not surprising that many special education teachers leave the field before their fifth year of teaching (Whitaker, 2003).

NCLB adds demands to the already difficult position of a special educator. To meet the NCLB requirements, special educators must be highly qualified in all subjects they teach. Although this is a logical goal for special educators, it is not an easy requirement to meet, especially at higher grade levels. Many special educators are responsible for teaching their students numerous subjects. Exceptional students who receive most of their education in the resource specialist program or a special day class program may receive anywhere from 1% to 99% of their instruction outside of the general education environment. Whereas most upper grade teachers specialize in one subject matter area, secondary-level special educators may need to specialize in several or all areas of subject matter. Therefore, the NCLB demands on special educators are higher than the demands on general educators (U.S. Department of Education & Office of Postsecondary Education, 2003).

The increase in demands on a field already suffering from personnel shortages will likely lead to even worse shortages. During the 1999–2000 school year, more than 12,000 special education positions were filled by unqualified personnel or remained vacant (Futrell, 2000). Higher salaries, adequate materials, and more involvement in decisions made in the workplace are some of the elements that would turn teaching into a more attractive profession (Futrell, 2000). However, special education would probably not be able to recruit enough teachers even if teaching children with disabilities became a more attractive profession (see Billingsley, 2004; Brownell et al., 2004).

It is especially important for special educators to be skilled in more than content knowledge. Special educators must also have effective skills in discipline, motivation, meeting individual differences, and writing individualized education programs (IEPs).

Competency tests need to evaluate all of these areas to ensure that teachers in the field can meet the demands of the profession (Whitaker, 2003). Zigmond (1997) observed:

> Special education was once worth receiving; it could be again. In many schools, it is not now. Here is where practitioners, policymakers, advocates, and researchers in special education need to focus—on defining the nature of special education and the competencies of the teachers who will deliver it. (p. 389)

The nature of special education and the competencies needed by special education teachers may be a matter of considerable debate, but Kauffman and Hallahan (2005) and Landrum and Kauffman (in press) have suggested both. Among the special competencies needed by special educators, according to Kauffman and his colleagues, are appropriate instructional modifications in pacing or rate, intensity, relentlessness, structure, reinforcement, pupil–teacher ratio, curriculum, and monitoring or assessment.

For teachers to gain the necessary skills to be successful with exceptional learners, more teacher educators are needed. However, enrollment in special education doctoral programs has declined 30% over the last 20 years (Pion, Smith, & Tyler, 2003). Due to this decline, some doctoral programs in special education have closed, and most special education doctoral programs are underenrolled. As enrollment is declining, a large portion of current special education professors are nearing retirement. Unless action is taken to increase the candidates for special education professorships, the NCLB requirement for preparation programs to produce highly qualified teachers will not be met (Pion et al., 2003; D. D. Smith, Pion, Tyler, & Gilmore, 2003; Tyler, Smith, & Pion, 2003).

To have highly qualified special educators, it is imperative that the pool of candidates be expanded. This pool of applicants could be increased by lowering the cost of teacher preparation and certification. Forgiveness loans could be given that would pay for 1 year of school in return for 1 year of teaching (Futrell, 2000).

An additional concern is raised by special educators who do not meet the demands of NCLB to be highly qualified. If teachers who do not meet this requirement are not allowed to continue teaching, this will result in larger class size. There will not be enough special educators in the field to keep class size down. Therefore, even if a class has a highly qualified teacher, the class size will be too large to meet the individual needs of students and increase student achievement. This change in class size would offset the purpose of requiring every special educator to be highly qualified (U.S. Department of Education & Office of Postsecondary Education, 2003).

THE AMBIGUOUS NCLB DEFINITION OF HIGHLY QUALIFIED PROFESSIONAL DEVELOPMENT

In addition to the requirement that every teacher be highly qualified, NCLB mandates that teachers receive high-quality professional development. Once again, the act provides a definition of high quality and steps for implementation, but both the definition and the steps are left ambiguous. If a program is to be provided across the United States, the necessary elements of the program must be clearly stated and understood. In addition, detailed steps on how to implement a specific program need to be provided to ensure that it will be implemented correctly across the nation (Cochran-Smith, 2002; U.S. Department of Education & Office of Postsecondary Education, 2003).

According to NCLB, high-quality professional development may involve various elements. These elements include partnerships with universities, opportunities to work with experienced teachers, and time to collaborate with professors. The definition leaves teacher educators with many questions. How can the partnerships be formed? What should occur in the partnerships with higher education? Where should the opportunities with experienced teachers take place? How much time should be given for collaboration with professors? If high-quality professional development is to be implemented appropriately across the United States, these questions must be answered. The role of universities must be defined, and the fact that university–school partnerships cannot be mandated by the federal government must be acknowledged. More guidance must be given for this goal to be achieved successfully (Cochran-Smith, 2002; U.S. Department of Education & Office of Postsecondary Education, 2003).

NCLB claims that research-based practice is an essential element of the demands it is placing on teachers and teacher educators. Yet, the changes required in NCLB to implement high-quality professional development are not currently supported by research evidence. This results in a mixed message (U.S. Department of Education & Office of Postsecondary Education, 2003).

A CLEAR ROAD MAP TO ACCOMPLISHMENT

Just as the definition of a highly qualified teacher must be federal, so must the steps to provide high-quality professional development. The development of high-quality professional development needs to be the primary focus of education (Hirsch, 1996).

For highly qualified professional development to be implemented, research evidence must be examined to determine the most successful model. In addition to implementing research-supported practices of professional development, a long-term commitment with realistic goals must be provided. The implementation of these elements will lead to the needed goal of highly qualified professional development (Lang & Fox, 2003).

Research has shown that longer, harder, and more thorough training leading to teachers' mastery of the skills on which they are being trained results in more effective teachers (Laczko-Kerr & Berliner, 2002). Therefore, it is imperative for teacher preparation programs to incorporate these aspects of preservice and in-service training.

Goals for professional development need to be appropriate and realistic. This does not mean we should lower educational expectations. It does mean that goals must be clear and not so lofty that they are unattainable. If the Department of Education truly wants to achieve the demands NCLB has set, then the goals and steps to achieve them must be clearly understood by those required to meet them.

If all teachers are to be highly qualified, then we must train teachers in what is known to result in better outcomes for students. There is a wealth of knowledge that has been found by researchers on what increases student gains, and teachers should understand and demonstrate competency in these practices (Youngs, Odden, & Porter, 2003). These practices must include the ability to integrate knowledge of students and content while planning instruction. Teachers need to be capable of analyzing student work and reflecting on instruction (Youngs et al., 2003).

Teacher preparation programs and school districts must educate future and current teachers on the importance of using research-based programs. Districts need to promote specific strategies and techniques that have been proven to work through research. If research-based practices are more widely adopted, then student outcomes will improve. A teacher who implements research-based practices might be considered highly qualified (Kauffman, 1993). However, we caution that a method found successful in a research program may fail in classroom implementation for a variety of reasons, including its unacceptability to teachers or lack of fidelity in implementation.

Teachers need to ignore what programs claim they can do and acknowledge what research has determined they can achieve. One program that has been researched extensively and found to be helpful for most students is direct instruction (Lloyd, 1975; Lloyd, Forness, & Kavale, 1998). This explicit, effective, and objective instruction is teacher directed. If a program has been determined to have a reliably positive effect on most children, then there is no question that all educators should be competent in this program.

Teachers must also use assessments to guide their instruction. Research evidence has shown that curriculum-based measurement (CBM) determines necessary instructional adjustments more effectively than other forms of assessment (Stecker & Fuchs, 2000). Highly qualified teachers would implement CBM with their students and use it as a guide for their instructional adjustments.

Educators lack classroom management skills. Teachers are entering the field of education without a thorough knowledge base in behavior management techniques and strategies that are successful with students. Teachers face the challenge of serving students with varying behavioral skills. Therefore, it is imperative that highly qualified teachers be skilled in working with varying behaviors (Lane, 2003).

Teacher preparation is an essential element of the education structure, but it needs to be improved. A study that analyzed the curricula of teacher education programs in prestigious schools of education found many areas in need of improvement (Keller, 2003a). The data revealed that many courses lacked rigor, practical techniques, and research-based methods. Educators must be equipped with an in-depth understanding of students and instructional strategies that meet their needs. Preparation for teaching students must be realistic, practical, and informative (Kauffman, 1994).

The realization that schools need to be good for teachers to be good for students will lead to better gains for students and an increase in the number of highly qualified teachers. The focus has always remained on the students, but we cannot ignore the needs of the teachers of these students. A highly qualified teacher will increase student outcomes, but this outcome cannot be expected if the conditions of teaching are extremely adverse. Educators need appropriate materials and support. These changes will enable teachers to increase student achievement and put their high qualification to good use (Kauffman, 2002).

Traditional professional development is not appropriate due to its fragmented approach on disconnected topics. Special educators need training with follow-up study groups and peer coaching teams to assist with implementation. Research has shown that the implementation rate is dramatically higher with this type of in-service than with the traditional approach (Lang & Fox, 2003).

We need additional research to discover the characteristics that make professional development highly effective. We cannot continue to enforce requirements that are not backed by research evidence, as this will not lead to greater gains for students. Investing in research is the only way to increase our knowledge of what creates effective professional development that produces more highly qualified teachers.

Many states may resist these changes because they will require additional funding, but it would be money well spent. The nation must require that states invest in these beneficial developments to create better student outcomes. In addition, although the changes needed for our educational system will cost more money in the beginning, in the long run if teachers are trained and supported appropriately, the turnover rate will decrease, which will inevitably lower costs of training and supporting new teachers (Goodlad, 1990).

The PCESE (2002) recommends that school districts "experiment" with various strategies to recruit and retain teachers. Recommending that school districts implement strategies nationwide before they have been found to be effective by research will not result in sufficient numbers of highly qualified special educators. Research must be done to determine which strategies are most effective and successful in increasing the candidate pool of teachers before school districts begin implementation. Moreover, if more highly qualified teachers are to be produced, then more good candidates for special education professorships must be identified and recruited.

Current financial support while attending a special education doctoral program is low. Researchers have found that an increase in financial support would allow more candidates to enter these doctoral programs. Evidence supports the idea that special education doctoral students should be recruited at a younger age to extend the time they serve as professors in the field. In addition, less than 50% of doctoral students in special education become professors (Hardman & West, 2003). Researchers indicate that incentives need to be increased to produce a larger percentage of doctoral students who become teacher educators (Hardman & West, 2003).

CONCLUSIONS

Improvement in teacher quality and professional development resulting from the various changes we have discussed will take time. There is no quick fix that will lead to greater student achievement. Only a realistic, long-term commitment and investment will result in better teachers, professional development, and student achievement (Kauffman, 1993). NCLB believes its requirements can be met by 2006. With all of the research and changes that need to occur, this does not appear to be realistic. The needed reform must start from a logical point, which is to focus on teacher education programs and professional development before requiring teachers to be highly qualified. Once highly qualified teacher education programs and professional development are in place, it is then appropriate to require teachers to gain competencies from these changes.

History has shown a pattern of abandonment of reforms (Kauffman, 1993, 2002; Kauffman & Landrum, in press). We are fearful that the NCLB reform will be merely another in this historical pattern if realistic and logical changes are not implemented. Only with appropriate changes, implementation, and support can NCLB increase teacher quality and professional development to produce improved student outcomes. However, this will not happen overnight, and it will happen only with appropriate definitions, logical steps, adequate resources, and sustained commitments (Kauffman, 2002).

REFERENCES

Berry, B., Hoke, M., & Hirsch, E. (2004). The search for highly qualified teachers. *Phi Delta Kappan, 85,* 684–689.

Billingsley, B. S. (2004). Special education teacher retention and attrition: A critical analysis of the research literature. *The Journal of Special Education, 38,* 39–55.

Brownell, M. T., Hirsch, E., & Seo, S. (2004). Meeting the demand for highly qualified special education teachers during severe shortages: What should policy makers consider? *The Journal of Special Education, 38,* 56–61.

Cochran-Smith, M. (2002). What a difference a definition makes: Highly qualified teachers, scientific research, and teacher education. *Journal of Teacher Education, 53,* 187–189.

Education Commission of the States. (2003). *Helping state leaders shape educational policy: Special education.* Denver, CO: Author. Retrieved October 25, 2003, from http://www.ecs.org/html/issue.asp?issueid =112

Elementary and Secondary Education Act. (2001). *No Child Left Behind Act of 2001.* Washington, DC: U.S. Department of Education. Retrieved October 27, 2003, from http://www.ed.gov/policy/elsec/leg/esea02/ beginning.html

Futrell, M. H. (2000). The challenge of the 21st century: Developing a highly qualified cadre of teachers to teach our nation's diverse student population. *Journal of Negro Education, 68,* 318–334.

Goodlad, J. I. (1990). *Teachers for our nation's schools.* San Francisco: Jossey-Bass.

Hardman, M. L., & West, J. (2003). Increasing the number of special education faculty: Policy implications and future directions. *Teacher Education and Special Education, 26,* 206–214.

Hirsch, E. D. (1996). *The schools we need and why we don't have them.* New York: Doubleday.

Kaplan, L. S., & Owings, W. A. (2003). No child left behind: The politics of teacher quality. *Phi Delta Kappan, 84,* 687–692.

Kauffman, J. M. (1993). How we might achieve the radical reform of special education. *Exceptional Children, 60,* 6–16.

Kauffman, J. M. (1994). Places of change: Special education's power and identity in an era of educational reform. *Journal of Learning Disabilities, 27,* 610–618.

Kauffman, J. M. (2002). *Education deform: Bright people sometimes say stupid things about education.* Lanham, MD: Scarecrow Education.

Kauffman, J. M., & Hallahan, D. P. (2005). *Special education: What it is and why we need it.* Boston: Allyn & Bacon.

Kauffman, J. M., & Landrum, T. J. (in press). *Children and youth with emotional and behavioral disorders: A brief history of their education.* Austin, TX: Pro-Ed.

Keller, B. (2003a, November 12). Education school courses faulted as intellectually thin. *Education Week.* Retrieved November 28, 2003, from http://www.edweek.org/ew/ewstory.cfm?slug=11Edschools.h23& tbstoryid=60

Keller, B. (2003b, October 29). States claim teachers are "qualified." *Education Week.* Retrieved November 9, 2003, from http://www.edweek.com/ew/ewstory.cfm?slug=09Qualified.h23

Laczko-Kerr, I., & Berliner, D. C. (2002, September 6). The effectiveness of "Teach for America" and other under-certified teachers on student academic achievement: A case of harmful public policy. *Education Policy Analysis Archives.* Retrieved October 28, 2003, from http://epaa.asu.edu/epaa/v10n37/

Landrum, T. J., & Kauffman, J. M. (in press). Educational service interventions and reforms. In J. W. Jacobson & J. A. Mulick (Eds.), *Handbook of mental retardation and developmental disabilities*. New York: Kluwer.

Lane, K. L. (2003). Identifying young students at risk for antisocial behavior: The utility of "teachers as tests." *Behavioral Disorders, 28*, 360–369.

Lang, M., & Fox, L. (2003). Breaking with tradition: Providing effective professional development for instructional personnel supporting students with severe disabilities. *Teacher Education and Special Education, 26*, 17–26.

Lloyd, J. (1975). The pedagogical orientation: An argument for improving instruction. *Journal of Learning Disabilities, 8*, 74–78.

Lloyd, J. W., Forness, S. R., & Kavale, K. A. (1998). Some methods are more effective than others. *Intervention in School and Clinic, 33*, 195–200.

McNergney, R. F., & Imig, S. R. (2003). Teacher evaluation. In J. W. Guthrie (Ed.), *Encyclopedia of education* (pp. 2453–2457). New York: Macmillan.

National Commission on Excellence in Education. (1983). *A nation at risk*. Washington, DC: U.S. Government Printing Office.

Pion, G. M., Smith, D. D., & Tyler, N. C. (2003). Career choices of recent doctorates in special education: Their implications for addressing faculty shortages. *Teacher Education and Special Education, 26*, 182–193.

President's Commission on Excellence in Special Education. (2002). *A new era: Revitalizing special education for children and their families*. Washington, DC: U.S. Department of Education. Retrieved October 27, 2003, from http://www.ed.gov/inits/commissionsboards/whspecialeducation/index.html

Rebell, M. A., & Hunter, M. A. (2004). "Highly qualified" teachers: Pretense or legal requirement. *Phi Delta Kappan, 85*, 690–696.

Smith, B. O. (1969). *Teachers for the real world*. Washington, DC: American Association of Colleges for Teacher Education.

Smith, B. O., Silverman, S. H., Borg, J. M., & Fry, B. V. (1980). *A design for a school of pedagogy*. Washington, DC: U.S. Department of Education.

Smith, D. D., Pion, G. M., Tyler, N. C., & Gilmore, R. (2003). Doctoral programs in special education: The nation's supplier. *Teacher Education and Special Education, 26*, 172–181.

Stecker, P. M., & Fuchs, L. S. (2000). Effecting superior achievement using curriculum-based measurement: The importance of individual progress monitoring. *Learning Disabilities Research & Practice, 15*, 128–134.

Tyler, N. C., Smith, D. D., & Pion, G. M. (2003). Doctoral students in special education: Characteristics and career aspirations. *Teacher Education and Special Education, 26*, 194–205.

U.S. Department of Education & Office of Postsecondary Education. (2003). *Meeting the highly qualified teachers challenge: The secretary's second annual report on teacher quality*. Washington, DC: Author.

Whitaker, S. D. (2003). Needs of beginning special education teachers: Implications for teacher education. *Teacher Education and Special Education, 26*, 106–117.

Youngs, P., Odden, A., & Porter, A. C. (2003). State policy related to teacher licensure. *Educational Policy, 17*, 217–237.

Zigmond, N. (1997). Educating students with disabilities: The future of special education. In J. W. Lloyd, E. J. Kame'enui, & D. Chard (Eds.), *Issues in educating students with disabilities* (pp. 377–390). Mahwah, NJ: Lawrence Erlbaum Associates, Inc.

EXCEPTIONALITY, *12*(4), 209–223

Comparisons of Traditionally and Alternatively Trained Teachers

Paul T. Sindelar, Ann Daunic, and Mary Sue Rennells

Department of Special Education
University of Florida

In this article, we present findings from a comparative study of 3 teacher preparation proto-types: traditional, university–district partnership, and district add-on programs. Samples of program graduates were observed during their 1st year of teaching using the Praxis III as-sessment. A larger sample completed a follow-up questionnaire assessing preparedness and efficacy, and a subset of them had principals submit ratings. On the observational measure, all teachers met minimum standards, but graduates of traditional programs outperformed their counterparts on several instructional criteria. By contrast, principals' ratings favored graduates of alternative programs, particularly partnership programs. These findings are discussed in terms of the distinction between formal and procedural knowledge, whereas differences between the 2 alternative pathways hint at the superiority of partnership pro-grams or other alternatives with equally rigorous content.

In special education, shortages of fully certified teachers have grown chronic and severe (McLeskey, Tyler, & Flippin, 2003). During 2001–2002, U.S. public schools employed nearly 49,000 teachers (of children ages 6–21) who were less than fully certified, over 12% of the workforce (U.S. Department of Education, n.d.-b). Among the roughly 31,000 teachers of preschool-aged children with disabilities, 4,201 (13.6%) were less than fully certified (U.S. Department of Education, n.d.-a). In response to these shortages and more recently to the No Child Left Behind (2001) mandate that all teachers be fully qualified by 2005–2006, alternatives to traditional teacher preparation are proliferating. Such alternatives are thought to help ameliorate teacher shortages in special education by providing access to teaching to individuals who did not and perhaps cannot enter teach-ing through traditional routes. In typical alternative route (AR) programs, coursework is abbreviated and field-based requirements are extended (Sindelar & Marks, 1993).

The idea of abbreviating pedagogical training evolved in the context of secondary teacher preparation, where, it was argued, subject matter mastery was as important if not more important than pedagogical training. Abbreviated programs were advocated for

---

Requests for reprints should be sent to Paul T. Sindelar, Department of Special Education, University of Florida, G-315 Norman Hall, Gainesville, FL 32611. E-mail: pts@coe.ufl.edu

midcareer changers with subject matter expertise (usually in mathematics and science) to expedite their entry into teaching. Concern also was expressed about the poor quality of teacher preparation courses and the possibility that they might actually discourage capable individuals from entering the field. No less an authority than the U.S. Department of Education (2002) advanced this argument, building on analyses of teacher quality research undertaken by the Abell Foundation (Walsh, 2001) and the Progressive Policy Institute (Hess, 2001).

Teacher education scholars in the secondary disciplines (e.g., Nathan & Petrosino, 2003) dispute this logic, of course, pointing out (among other things) that having expert knowledge does not guarantee the ability to represent it in a meaningful way for developing learners. Moreover, for elementary and special education, this logic simply does not fit well. Teaching younger children requires both subject mastery and pedagogical knowledge, and when children do not learn readily, pedagogical knowledge becomes increasingly important. Furthermore, in contrast to teacher preparation in secondary fields, elementary and special education programs typically require more credit hours (Galambos, Cornett, & Spitler, 1985). Thus, the tendency for AR programs to abbreviate course requirements may serve to dilute—and not improve—the quality of special education teacher education.

In a recent review of research on the outcomes of AR programs, Rosenberg and Sindelar (2001) found only seven studies of special education teacher preparation. Although these studies generally reported favorable outcomes for AR programs, Rosenberg and Sindelar noted that most of them were not abbreviated. To the contrary, successful special education AR programs were characterized by rigorous, coherent content and substantial length. These authors also noted that collaboration among program providers and frequent, meaningful supervision also contributed to program success.

Their conclusions parallel those of researchers in general teacher preparation (Zeichner & Schulte, 2001), and some consensus about AR preparation seems to be emerging in the field. That consensus begins with the proposition that AR preparation applies to a large set of heterogeneous programs—so heterogeneous, in fact, that they no longer may be thought of fruitfully as constituting a single class. Programs—including traditional programs—are more appropriately described by careful delineation of elements than by broad brushstrokes like "alternative" or "traditional" route. There also is emerging consensus about empirical findings, which suggest that ARs can produce effective teachers, particularly when certain program elements—meaningful methods courses, field experience, supervision, and mentorship—are in place. They also have proven successful (particularly in urban areas) in attracting culturally and linguistically diverse candidates (Zeichner & Schulte, 2001). On the other hand, consensus also holds that fast-track programs—programs that rapidly move inexperienced trainees into teaching positions without extensive preparation—are often lacking critical programmatic elements, and research has shown them to be highly costly (Darling-Hammond, 2000).

Thus, what research has taught us about alternative preparation routes applies best to the extremes of the AR continuum, to programs most and least like traditional campus-based preservice training. The notion that not all AR programs are alike has stirred demand for additional research in which program variants are compared. Such research will help policymakers determine what prototypes offer the most promise and inform program designers about essential elements of program structure and organization. In this article, we report findings from one such study in special education. We compared graduates of traditional programs to graduates (or completers) of two types of alternative programs: university–district degree program partnerships (ALT 1, or partnership programs) and district add-on programs (ALT 2, or add-on programs). We studied graduates of four traditional programs, three partnership programs, and three add-on programs, all in Florida. The purpose of the study was to compare graduates of these three program prototypes on observations of classroom performance, principals' ratings, feelings of preparedness, and sense of efficacy.

METHOD

In this section, we describe how we conducted classroom observations and how we obtained principal ratings and teacher self-reports.

Classroom Observations

For classroom observations, we used *Praxis III: Classroom Performance Assessments of the Praxis Series: Professional Assessments for Beginning Teachers*™. Praxis is a comprehensive assessment system developed by the Educational Testing Service (ETS; Dwyer, 1994). The first two components of the series are designed to assess basic skills and knowledge of subject matter and pedagogy. The third component, Praxis III, is designed to assess application of this knowledge in the classroom, typically toward the end of an internship experience or during the first year of teaching. Its original purpose was to assist states that require a performance-based assessment as part of their licensing procedures.

In describing the instrument, Dwyer and Villegas (1993) emphasized assessment of teacher actions and judgments within the context of the classroom. Although Praxis III is predominantly performance based, paper-and-pencil tasks are included to enable teachers to describe the classroom and instructional arrangements. In pre- and postobservation interviews, teachers have the opportunity to explain their instructional decisions in light of their grasp of the subject matter, the principles of learning and teaching, and the individual backgrounds of their pupils.

The 19 measurement criteria that constitute Praxis III were developed from extensive research (Reynolds, 1992), the results of three job analyses, and a multistate validity study (Dwyer, 1993, 1994). They were piloted extensively in the field and refined in collaboration with practicing educators. The criteria are organized into four domains of teacher competence. These domains, with the corresponding criteria defined by ETS (Dwyer & Villegas, 1993), are displayed in Table 1.

The assessment cycle.   Prior to the preobservation interview, an assessor provides each participant with three assessment profiles: (a) a candidate profile that asks for information about the participant's educational background and experience, (b) a classroom profile that asks for information about demographic and academic characteristics

TABLE 1
Praxis III Domains and Criteria (Dwyer & Villegas, 1993)

Domain A: Organizing content knowledge for student learning
  1. Becoming familiar with students' backgrounds
  2. Articulating learning goals
  3. Understanding connections among past, current, and future content
  4. Selecting appropriate methods, activities, and materials
  5. Selecting appropriate evaluation strategies
Domain B: Creating an environment for student learning
  1. Creating a climate that promotes fairness
  2. Establishing rapport
  3. Communicating challenging expectations
  4. Establishing consistent standards of behavior
  5. Making the physical environment safe and conducive to learning
Domain C: Teaching for student learning
  1. Making goals and procedures clear
  2. Making content comprehensible
  3. Encouraging extension of thinking
  4. Monitoring student learning and providing feedback
  5. Using class time effectively
Domain D: Teacher professionalism
  1. Reflecting on student learning
  2. Demonstrating sense of efficacy
  3. Building professional relationships
  4. Communicating with parents

of the students in the class to be observed, and (c) an instruction profile that asks for information about the lesson. The participating teacher is asked to reflect on lesson planning in terms of goals, relation to past and future learning, methods, materials, and means of student evaluation.

In the preobservation interview, the assessor provides the participant an opportunity to explain the lesson-planning process and why particular goals and methods were chosen. In the postobservation interview, the participant is provided an opportunity to reflect on what happened during the lesson and how this information could enhance future planning. The assessor also asks about methods of communication with parents or guardians and relationships with fellow professionals.

The time required for an assessment cycle may vary but generally falls within predictable guidelines. Following a 20- to 30-min preobservation interview, the assessor observes the lesson described in the instruction profile, which may last from 20 min to 1 hr, depending on lesson content, grade level, and student characteristics. As soon as possible after the classroom observation, the assessor interviews the beginning teacher again; this postobservation interview typically requires from 30 to 40 min.

Following completion of the assessment cycle, the assessor reviews the teacher-prepared written documents and all notes taken during the three phases. The notes and questionnaire (document) responses are coded according to relevant criteria; evidence for each assessment criterion may be drawn from any of the data sources. After coding, the assessor (a) transfers pertinent information for each criterion to the record of evidence,

(b) relates the evidence to the criterion's specified scoring rules with a written statement, and (c) assigns a score. Criterion scores range from 1.0 to 3.5 at intervals of 0.5. The scoring process typically takes 1 to 1.5 hr for each of the four domains. (Each domain includes four or five criteria.) Assessors can refer to written descriptions of criteria and guiding questions prepared by ETS, but they also must rely on judgments informed by their own experience and by a rigorous Praxis III assessor training procedure.

Assessor training.   Praxis III is a high-inference instrument. Assessors are asked to consider each participant's teaching context (i.e., grade level, subject, and student characteristics) and to draw on their own experience to judge the evidence they collect. Therefore, each assessor must complete a weeklong interactive training workshop that incorporates videotapes, the examination of printed materials, and multiple simulated assessments. Throughout the first 4 days, participants receive feedback from instructors and colleagues. They then must conduct a field test using Praxis III and return for the fifth day of the workshop. Trainers provide additional feedback, reinforce skills, consolidate learning, and assess participants on the full range of Praxis III activities.

Potential assessors are cautioned that there is a wide range of acceptable teaching styles, even though a particular style may not match an assessor's individual preference. Moreover, Praxis III trainers emphasize the importance of not penalizing beginning teachers for circumstances that may be beyond their control (e.g., class size, building facilities, or lack of resources). Thus, assessors are to use informed judgments while adhering closely to the scoring rules for each criterion. In our study, four research assistants, all doctoral students in special education or school psychology, were trained in use of Praxis III by ETS trainers.

Reliability and validity.   A preliminary analysis of data collected during field testing indicated a moderate to high level of interrater agreement between paired assessors who observed the same teaching event (Dwyer, 1994). However, no interrater reliability data have been published to date. ETS does not emphasize the importance of interrater reliability; rather, they stress the importance of using highly trained assessors. Ultimately, therefore, the reliability and validity of Praxis III rests in the rigor of the assessor training (Villegas, 1992).

Principals' Ratings and Teachers' Self-Reports

We developed two rating forms, one for graduates' principals (the Principal Questionnaire [PQ]) and one for graduates themselves (the Graduate Questionnaire [GQ]). On the PQ, principals were asked to rate teachers on 20 items keyed to Praxis III criteria. (One Praxis criterion was subdivided, and one was eliminated.) As a result, it was possible to determine principals' assessments of graduates' strengths and weaknesses on 18 of the 19 Praxis criteria. All items used different 7-point Likert scales.

On the GQ, we assessed program graduates' sense of preparedness and efficacy. Preparedness was assessed on a series of 22 Likert items scored on a 7-point scale ranging from 1 (*prepared me poorly*) to 7 (*prepared me well*), covering instruction, evaluation and data use, classroom management, and special education procedures. The efficacy scale comprised 16 items, most adopted from other efficacy scales, on which respondents were asked to characterize their agreement on a scale of 1 (*strongly disagree*) to 6 (*strongly agree*).

Participant Selection

Observations.   We identified all beginning public school special education teachers who completed one of the six AR programs or who had graduated from one of the four state university programs participating in the study. To be included in the sample, participants were required to be teaching in the state of Florida in their areas of certification. To limit the number of traditional program graduates, approximately 10 teachers from each of the four state universities were selected through a stratified random sampling procedure.

We sent letters to all beginning teachers included in the sample informing them that they had been selected for an important research study and asking them to participate. Letters were followed with phone calls until samples of 4 graduates from each traditional program (a total of 16), 15 graduates of ALT 1 (partnership) programs, and 15 teachers who completed ALT 2 (add-on) programs were obtained.

Principals' ratings and self-reports of preparedness and efficacy.   To identify a sample, we obtained from the Florida Department of Education a list of beginning teachers and the districts in which they were employed. The list provided names, areas of certification, district and school of employment, job code descriptions, and number of teaching years. This information was necessary for matching graduates with teacher education programs as well as ensuring that job descriptions corresponded with areas of certification. We mailed GQs and PQs to all cohort members from the 10 participating programs.

We asked graduates to complete the GQ and to ask their principals to complete the PQ. We sent follow-up postcards about 3 weeks later and 2 weeks after that made follow-up telephone calls to all teachers from whom we had still received no response. Once a teacher's permission was obtained (either verbally or in writing), follow-up was conducted with their principals via telephone calls. Principals' participation was solicited, and consenting principals were offered the option to complete the questionnaire over the phone or to receive the questionnaire in the mail. Four principals completed the PQ over the phone, and the rest returned the PQ in the mail.

GQs and PQs were initially mailed to 288 graduates. Of those, 126 graduates either could not be contacted or did not wish to participate. Ninety-two of the remaining 162 PQs were completed and returned by graduates' principals, yielding a 56.79% total return rate. The return rates for individual program types were (a) 65.9% ($n = 58$ questionnaires returned) for traditional, (b) 60.5% ($n = 23$ questionnaires returned) for ALT 1, and (c) 35.4% ($n = 11$ questionnaires returned) for ALT 2.

RESULTS

This section is divided into three parts: participant demographics, observational data, and ratings and self-reports.

Participant Demographics

As expected, traditional program participants were younger ($M = 24.5$ years) than either the ALT 1 ($M = 34.6$ years) or ALT 2 ($M = 39.0$ years) participants. Almost all participants were women, and although most were White, the alternative programs had higher percentages of non-White participants. In fact, 46% of ALT 2 participants were African American, Hispanic, Native American, or Haitian. Traditional program participants were more likely to describe their parents as college graduates; parents of AR participants were likely to have completed high school but to have gone no further in school.

As expected, few traditional program participants held teaching certificates ($M = 2\%$). By contrast, 42% of participants in ALT 1 and 100% of ALT 2 programs were certified. (Participants in ALT 2 programs were required to be certified.) Whereas more than half of the traditional (59%) and ALT 1 (62%) participants anticipated that special education teaching would be their lifelong career, only 40% of the ALT 2 participants did so. The percentage of participants who expected to teach special education no more than 3 years was small and comparable across programs.

Observational Data

Analysis.   Scores on each of the 19 Praxis III assessment criteria, the four domain summary scores, and the total Praxis III assessment score were submitted to a one-way between-subjects multivariate analysis of variance (MANOVA) with type of program as the grouping variable. Type of program was characterized as either ALT 1 ($n = 15$), ALT 2 ($n = 15$), or traditional ($n = 16$). Univariate analyses of variance (ANOVAs) were conducted to determine the specific criteria or group domains on which groups differed. To guarantee adequate statistical power, alpha was set at .10 for all analyses.

Findings.   In Tables 2 through 5, for each program type, we report mean scores and standard deviations for each criterion by domain. Scores ranged from 1.0 to 3.5 and averaged 2.25. According to ETS, a score of 2.0 designates minimum competence on a criterion or domain. In these tables, we also report the results on univariate

TABLE 2
Means and Standard Deviations for Praxis III Ratings
on Domain A Criteria by Group

Criterion	Traditional		ALT 1		ALT 2		F
	M	SD	M	SD	M	SD	
A1	2.75	0.45	2.67	0.36	2.23	0.50	6.11**
A2	2.41	0.58	2.17	0.67	2.27	0.73	0.51
A3	2.06	0.36	2.03	0.58	2.03	0.64	0.02
A4	2.72	0.36	2.43	0.46	2.37	0.64	0.86
A5	2.13	0.56	1.90	0.39	2.00	0.46	0.86
Summary score	12.06	1.55	11.20	1.27	10.90	2.01	2.13

**$p < .05$.

TABLE 3
Means and Standard Deviations for Praxis III Ratings on Domain B Criteria by Group

Criterion	Traditional M	Traditional SD	ALT 1 M	ALT 1 SD	ALT 2 M	ALT 2 SD	F
B1	2.60	0.52	2.53	0.55	2.08	0.56	4.26**
B2	2.78	0.52	2.80	0.41	2.53	0.61	1.24
B3	2.56	0.60	2.57	0.59	2.53	0.83	0.01
B4	3.13	0.29	2.90	0.39	2.87	0.48	2.02
B5	2.66	0.47	2.70	0.53	2.67	0.56	0.03
Summary score	13.72	1.74	12.50	2.04	12.67	2.32	1.13

**$p < .05$.

TABLE 4
Means and Standard Deviations for Praxis III Ratings on Domain C Criteria by Group

Criterion	Traditional M	Traditional SD	ALT 1 M	ALT 1 SD	ALT 2 M	ALT 2 SD	F
C1	2.44	0.57	1.97	0.44	2.07	0.65	3.04*
C2	2.63	0.56	2.20	0.53	2.23	0.65	2.58*
C3	1.84	0.51	1.93	0.46	1.87	0.72	0.10
C4	2.91	0.27	2.47	0.58	2.47	0.58	4.10**
C5	2.59	0.46	2.67	0.56	2.33	0.62	1.56
Summary score	12.41	1.59	11.23	1.70	10.97	2.26	2.63*

*$p < .10$. **$p < .05$.

TABLE 5
Means and Standard Deviations for Praxis III Ratings on Domain D Criteria by Group

Criterion	Traditional M	Traditional SD	ALT 1 M	ALT 1 SD	ALT 2 M	ALT 2 SD	F
D1	2.53	0.53	2.27	0.59	2.27	0.73	0.95
D2	2.75	0.41	2.47	0.44	2.40	0.57	2.36
D3	2.66	0.47	3.00	0.38	2.57	0.59	3.29**
D4	2.56	0.44	2.53	0.52	2.37	0.58	2.52*
Summary score	10.50	0.88	10.27	1.03	9.60	1.48	2.97*
Total score	48.69	4.53	46.20	4.37	44.13	6.52	2.97*

*$p < .10$. **$p < .05$.

ANOVAs, which we used to follow up the significant overall MANOVA, Hotelling's $F(38, 48) = 1.866$, $p = .021$.

The univariate ANOVAs yielded the following results: On six Praxis III criteria—becoming familiar with relevant aspects of students' background and experiences (A1), creating a climate that promotes fairness (B1), making learning goals and instructional procedures clear to students (C1), making content comprehensible to students (C2), monitoring students' understanding of content, providing feedback, and adjusting learning activities (C4), and building professional relationships (D3)—differences were found among the three groups of teachers.

Follow-up tests (using Tukey's Studentized Range) to determine the direction of significant differences revealed the following: On Criteria A1 and B1, the mean scores for graduates of traditional and ALT 1 programs, which did not differ, were significantly higher than the means for ALT 2 participants. On Criteria C1, C2, and C4, the traditional group mean was significantly higher than the means of either AR group. On Criterion D3, the ALT 1 group scored significantly higher than did either the traditional or ALT 2 groups.

Univariate ANOVAs also yielded significant differences for the summary score for Domain C (Teaching for Student Learning), the summary score for Domain D (Teacher Professionalism), and for the total Praxis score (the mean for all 19 criteria). Follow-up tests revealed that on Domain C and the Praxis total score, the traditional program graduates scored higher than did graduates of both AR groups. On Domain D, however, the traditional program graduates and the ALT 1 group, which did not differ, scored higher than did ALT 2 program participants.

Principals' Ratings and Self-Reports

In Tables 6 through 9, we report item-by-item means, standard deviations, and F values by program type and corresponding Praxis III domain. As these data show, principals consistently rated graduates of partnership programs as highly competent. ALT 1 mean scores on the 20 PQ items ranged from 6.13 to 6.65. Principals also assigned high ratings to ALT 2 graduates. Their average scores on the 20 PQ items ranged from 5.55 to 6.55. Principals ranked traditional graduates lower; their scores ranged from 5.41 to 6.29.

TABLE 6
Means and Standard Deviations for Principals' Ratings
on Domain A Criteria by Group

| Criterion | Traditional | | ALT 1 | | ALT 2 | | |
	M	SD	M	SD	M	SD	F
A1	5.41	1.04	6.13	0.36	5.82	0.50	4.36**
A2	5.60	1.14	6.22	0.67	5.82	1.47	2.63
A3	5.50	1.06	6.17	0.65	5.82	1.40	3.64**
A5	5.53	1.17	6.39	0.66	6.00	1.48	5.09**

Note. No item for Praxis III Criterion A4 was developed.
**$p < .05$.

TABLE 7
Means and Standard Deviations for Principals' Ratings on Domain B Criteria by Group

Criterion	Traditional M	SD	ALT 1 M	SD	ALT 2 M	SD	F
B1	6.29	1.04	6.65	0.49	6.36	0.92	1.25
B2	6.10	1.09	6.61	0.58	6.27	1.01	2.20
B3	5.60	1.12	6.26	0.62	5.82	1.47	3.11**
B4	5.71	1.21	6.36	0.66	6.27	1.56	3.12**
B5	6.02	1.12	6.37	0.50	6.55	0.69	4.00**

**$p < .05$.

TABLE 8
Means and Standard Deviations for Principals' Ratings on Domain C Criteria by Group

Criterion	Traditional M	SD	ALT 1 M	SD	ALT 2 M	SD	F
C1	5.85	1.14	6.39	0.58	6.09	1.22	2.32
C2	5.76	1.08	6.39	0.58	5.91	1.45	3.09
C3	5.59	1.09	6.18	0.80	6.09	1.14	3.17***
C4a	5.53	1.05	6.14	0.64	6.00	1.34	3.29**
C4b	5.76	1.03	6.41	0.67	6.09	1.38	3.45**
C4c	5.67	1.16	6.41	0.67	5.91	1.58	3.10**
C5	5.60	1.17	6.55	0.60	5.82	1.54	5.72**

**$p < .05$. ***$p < .05$, but no significant follow-up tests.

TABLE 9
Means and Standard Deviations for Principals' Ratings on Domain D Criteria by Group

Criterion	Traditional M	SD	ALT 1 M	SD	ALT 2 M	SD	F
D1	5.29	0.90	6.18	0.66	5.73	1.79	6.51**
D2	5.72	1.12	6.46	0.67	6.55	0.69	5.50**
D3	5.86	1.07	6.46	0.60	5.55	1.70	3.41***
D4	5.81	1.03	6.55	0.51	6.09	1.30	4.59**

**$p < .05$. ***$p < .05$, but no significant follow-up tests.

Average item scores on the PQ were compared by program type (ALT 1, ALT 2, and traditional) using ANOVA. Significant overall F values (with $p < .05$) were followed up using Tukey's Studentized Range procedure. For three significant F values, this follow-up procedure yielded no significant differences among the groups. When significant differences were obtained on the follow-up tests, ALT 1 graduates consistently received significantly higher ratings than traditional graduates, ALT 2 scores did not differ significantly from ALT 1 scores, and ALT 2 scores did not differ significantly from traditional scores, on any item.

Principals' ratings of ALT 1 graduates were significantly greater than traditional graduates' ratings on three of four Domain A items (familiarizing oneself with relevant aspects of students' backgrounds; drawing connections among content learned previously, current content, and future content; and selecting appropriate evaluation strategies), two items in Domain B (communicating challenging learning expectations to students, and making the physical environment safe and conducive to learning), four items in Domain C (related to two criteria—monitoring understanding, providing feedback, adjusting instruction; and using instructional time effectively), and three items in Domain D (reflecting on student learning, demonstrating a sense of efficacy, and communicating with parents).

GQ preparedness scale.   Univariate ANOVAs revealed significant differences among the three program types on 8 of the 22 preparedness items. Follow-up tests (again using Tukey's Studentized Range procedure) were then conducted to determine the direction of these differences. Traditional participants' mean scores ranged from 3.21 to 5.59, ALT 1 participants' mean scores ranged from 3.95 to 5.95, and ALT 2 participants' mean scores ranged from 4.16 to 5.70. On evaluation items, scores for ALT 1 programs were significantly higher than the mean scores for traditional programs. Both ALT 1 and ALT 2 program means also exceeded traditional means on items we construed to assess procedural knowledge—that is, knowledge of school and classroom procedures and routines. On all but one item, the groups did not differ on instructional preparedness, and they felt equally well prepared to manage behavior and meet students' needs.

GQ efficacy scale.   Graduates of traditional, ALT 1, and ALT 2 programs all expressed a healthy sense of professional efficacy. Graduates of traditional programs averaged 3.03 to 5.29, ALT 1 graduates averaged 3.65 to 5.36, and ALT 2 graduates averaged 2.90 to 5.47. Only one item on the efficacy scale—the amount that a student can learn, which is primarily related to family background—differentiated among the groups so that the traditional and ALT 1 groups reported greater agreement with the statement than ALT 2 graduates.

DISCUSSION

All teachers, regardless of the nature of their preparation, exhibited at least basic competence on almost all of the Praxis III criteria. Only on Criterion C3—encouraging students to extend their thinking—did each of the three groups average below the 2.0 standard of minimum competence. Thus, despite differences among the groups on specific criteria, all three program types appeared capable of producing graduates who are competent beginning teachers.

Differences among the three groups of teachers are noteworthy. Traditional program graduates outperformed teachers who completed both types of AR programs on three criteria in Domain C—making goals and instructional procedures clear to students (C1), making content comprehensible (C2), and monitoring student learning and providing appropriate feedback (C4). The traditional graduates also scored better on the Domain C summary score and on the total Praxis III score. Domain C—Teaching for Student Learning—encompasses skills in accomplishing the teacher's goals for imparting lesson content to his or her students. It entails connecting that content to the individual and collective experiences of the students and engaging them in the learning process. It is what we commonly consider the heart of teaching.

On Criteria A1, becoming familiar with relevant aspects of students' background knowledge and experience; B1, fairness; and on the summary score for Domain D, Teacher Professionalism, graduates of university–district partnership programs and traditional university graduates outperformed teachers who completed district add-on training. High scores on Criteria A1 and B1 indicate awareness of the importance of attending to students as individuals and providing all students with access to learning. It may be that participants who completed district add-on programs were more likely to have had a prior orientation in general education with less emphasis on individualization. In addition, graduates of degree-granting programs (both traditional and university–district collaborations) may have been more attuned to individualized approaches because of a greater amount of coursework. Indeed, we had established in analyses of interview data that faculty in traditional and ALT 1 programs were more concerned about the sequence and organization of program requirements, whereas faculty at ALT 2 programs were more pragmatic about requirements and how they were sequenced.

The higher Domain D summary score of traditional and ALT 1 program graduates reflects the relatively high scores of traditional graduates across all criteria in Domain D and the particularly high score of ALT 1 participants on Criterion D3, building professional relationships. On D3, ALT 1 graduates outscored both the traditional and the ALT 2 groups. Two of these programs were designed for paraprofessionals, so graduates had had ample opportunity to communicate and establish relationships with school professionals.

Although differences among the groups were evidenced on several criteria and summary scores, the relative strengths and weaknesses for participants within each program type follow a somewhat similar pattern. When domain averages are considered, all teachers tended to exhibit stronger skills in Domain B (Creating an Environment for Student Learning) and Domain D (Teacher Professionalism) and weaker skills in Domain A (Organizing Content Knowledge for Student Learning) and Domain C (Teaching for Student Learning). Regarding individual criteria within these domains, teachers from all groups were relatively strong on building rapport (B2) and establishing consistent standards for behavior (B4). They were relatively weak on extending students' thinking (C3); understanding the connections among previous, current, and future content (A3); and selecting appropriate evaluation strategies (A5). These findings are consistent with analyses of teacher development that suggest novices first develop organizational and management skills before turning their attention to curriculum and instruction.

The Praxis III assessment system was designed for and field-tested with general education teachers. We were interested in how appropriate the instrument would be for the special education environments represented by the classrooms observed in this study. We were favorably impressed by the adaptability of the Praxis III assessment. Our experience supported its use in a variety of classroom contexts and its utility for assessing teachers in special education. Moreover, the patterns of relative strengths and weaknesses evidenced by all three groups of teachers across the 19 Praxis III criteria help substantiate our impressions. For example, it seems logical that beginning special education teachers would be relatively more skilled in criteria related to maintaining standards of behavior and establishing rapport with students and would be relatively weaker on criteria related to a thorough understanding of content, including the selection of appropriate evaluation strategies. The historical emphasis in special education on the enhancement of basic skills also is consistent with the finding that all three groups of teachers scored lowest in encouraging students to extend their thinking.

One word of caution in interpreting the competence level of all program participants is warranted: Because all were volunteers, we are unable to draw general conclusions about program effectiveness. Although this caveat holds equally across all three program types and therefore should not affect the validity of intergroup comparisons, it may be a contributing factor to participants' generally positive ratings. It seems circumspect to say that these group averages may be overestimated somewhat.

It is interesting to note that despite differences generally favoring traditionally trained teachers on observational measures, the same group fared worst in the eyes of their principals. Both groups of alternatively trained teachers were rated higher by their principals on every Praxis criterion (with the exception of D3, professional relationships, on which ALT 2 teachers were rated lower than traditionally trained teachers). The differences between the ALT 1 and traditional teachers' ratings were statistically significant on 12 of 20 items.

The discrepancy between observational and principals' rating data call into question the validity of the latter, and Praxis Criterion C3—extends students' thinking—makes this point perfectly. The observational data suggest that the performance of all three groups of teachers was substandard on this criterion (and that there were no significant differences among the groups). On the same criterion, however, principals rated all of the groups at least above average. Principals' ratings of traditionally trained teachers averaged 5.58 on a 7-point scale, and the average scores of the two AR groups exceeded 6. On a similar item on the GQ, the beginning teachers rated themselves only slightly above average.

Clearly, principals were not rating the same phenomena our observers were, and it may be unfair to ask them for accurate judgments of precisely defined performances. Their ratings may be better understood as relative group rankings. In this sense, it seems logical that principals would prefer AR graduates to traditional graduates because the former have far more understanding of how schools operate than do the latter (and so present fewer problems to their principals). Given the particular nature of the two AR program types, it also seems reasonable that principals would prefer graduates of ALT 1 to ALT 2 program completers. Many graduates of partnership programs worked as paraprofessionals in the same schools where they were hired to teach. Perhaps it is fairest to say that principals may have based their ratings on teachers' procedural knowledge (about the school and district). Traditional graduates cannot be expected to enter a school with the same savvy as an experienced teacher or paraprofessional. However, our observational findings suggest that they do bring more formal knowledge to the job, particularly of instruction, than do their AR counterparts.

Finally, we found the Praxis III assessment to provide a clear and coherent picture of the competence of teachers who participated in this study despite the fact that Praxis III was designed to assess general education teachers. Praxis scores allowed for quantitative comparisons of participant groups on individual criteria and domains of teaching; they also provided qualitative data on each participant observed through the records of evidence gathered by assessors.

Most important, however, Praxis scores differentiated among groups in meaningful ways. Differences favoring traditionally trained teachers could be related to their relative mastery of formal knowledge (of instruction), and differences favoring graduates of partnership programs could be related to their having worked as paraprofessionals in the schools where they now taught. Our observational findings, taken together with principals' ratings, suggest that between the two AR program prototypes, university–district partnership programs were more effective. Compared to district add-on programs, they prepared better and more committed teachers. That the former were typically longer and more coherent than the latter affirms generalizations about the relative effectiveness of AR programs drawn from previous research.

ACKNOWLEDGMENTS

We thank Candace Austrich, Mary Eisele, and Karen Kuhel for their contributions on earlier versions of this article.

REFERENCES

Darling-Hammond, L. (2000). *Solving the dilemmas of teacher supply, demand, and standards: How we can ensure a competent, caring, and qualified teacher for every child.* New York: National Commission on Teaching and America's Future.

Dwyer, C. A. (1993). Teaching and diversity: Meeting the challenges for innovative teacher assessments. *Journal of Teacher Education, 44,* 119–129.

Dwyer, C. A. (1994). *Development of the knowledge base for the Praxis III: Classroom performance assessments assessment criteria.* Princeton, NJ: Educational Testing Service.

Dwyer, C. A., & Villegas, A. M. (1993). *Guiding conceptions and assessment principles for the Praxis series: Professional assessments for beginning teachers* (Research Rep. No. 93–17). Princeton, NJ: Educational Testing Service.

Galambos, E. C., Cornett, L. M., & Spitler, H. D. (1985). *An analysis of transcripts of teachers and arts and sciences graduates.* Atlanta, GA: Southern Regional Educational Board. (ERIC Document Reproduction Service No. 257 82)

Hess, F. M. (2001). *Tear down this wall: The case for a radical overhaul of teacher certification.* Washington, DC: Progressive Policy Institute. Retrieved May 11, 2004, from http://www.ppionline.org/documents/teacher_certification.pdf

McLeskey, J., Tyler, N., & Flippin, S. (2003). *The supply and demand for special education teachers: A review of research regarding the nature of the chronic shortage of special education* (COPSSE Document No. RS–1). Gainesville: University of Florida, Center on Personnel Studies in Special Education.

Nathan, M. J., & Petrosino, A. (2003). Expert blind spot among preservice teachers. *American Educational Research Journal, 40,* 905–928.

No Child Left Behind Act. Reauthorization of the Elementary and Secondary Education Act, Pub. L. No. 107–110, 2102(4) (2001).

Reynolds, A. (1992). What is competent beginning teaching? A review of the literature. *Review of Education Research, 62,* 1–35.

Rosenberg, M. S., & Sindelar, P. T. (2001). *The proliferation of alternative routes to certification in special education: A critical review of the literature.* Arlington, VA: National Clearinghouse for Professions in Special Education, The Council for Exceptional Children. Retrieved May 10, 2004, from http://www.special-ed-careers.org

Sindelar, P. T., & Marks, L. J. (1993). Alternative route programs: Implications for elementary and special education. *Teacher Education and Special Education, 16,* 146–154.

U.S. Department of Education. (2002). *Meeting the highly qualified teachers challenge: The Secretary's annual report on teacher quality: 2002.* Washington, DC: Author.

U.S. Department of Education. (n.d.-a). *Table AC1: Number of special education teachers serving students ages 3–5, by state.* Washington, DC: Author. Retrieved May 10, 2004, from http://www.ideadata.org/arc_toc4.asp#partbPEN

U.S. Department of Education. (n.d.-b). *Table AC2: Number of special education teachers serving students ages 6–21, by state.* Washington, DC: Author. Retrieved May 10, 2004, from http://www.ideadata.org/arc_toc4.asp#partbPEN

Villegas, A. M. (1992, February). *The competence needed by beginning teachers in a multicultural society.* Paper presented at the annual meeting of the American Association of Colleges of Teacher Education, San Antonio, TX.

Walsh, K. (2001). *Teacher certification reconsidered: Stumbling for quality.* Baltimore: Abell Foundation. Retrieved May 11, 2004, from http://www.abell.org/publications/detail.asp?ID=59

Zeichner, K. M., & Schulte, A. K. (2001). What we know and don't know from peer-reviewed research about alternative teacher certification programs. *Journal of Teacher Education, 52,* 266–282.

EXCEPTIONALITY, *12*(4), 225–238

Alternatively Licensing Career Changers To Be Teachers in the Field of Special Education: Their First-Year Reflections

Laurie U. deBettencourt and Lori Howard
School of Continuing and Professional Studies
University of Virginia

Although many areas in education are experiencing teacher shortages, shortages of teachers who are qualified in the area of special education are of critical concern. This article describes a federally funded training program to alternatively license special education teachers. Fifty-nine career changers participated. They taught special education in 2 southeastern school districts and were surveyed 3 times during their 1st year of teaching. Their reflections on the training program, their school district mentors, and their teaching experiences are discussed. As all alternative licensure training programs are not the same, this article begins to document several components of 1 program.

Although many areas in education are experiencing teacher shortages, the shortages of teachers who are qualified in the area of special education are of critical concern (Billingsley & McLeskey, 2004; Brownell, Sindelar, Bishop, Langley, & Seo, 2002; McLeskey, Tyler, & Flippin, 2004; Pipho, 1998). Although a recent federal mandate for highly qualified teachers has the potential for increasing the number of certified special education teachers (Billingsley & McLeskey, 2004), it also has the potential for exacerbating the shortage. The mandate requires content area certification and suggests that secondary teachers are required to be certified both in special education and in the content area they teach. This requirement could increase the shortage of special education teachers. In addition, a number of other factors have created special education teacher shortages. A growing number of students in need of special services (U.S. Department of Education, 2001), an increase in special education caseloads (Billingsley & McLeskey, 2004), and the departure of special education teachers from the teaching profession (Billingsley, 2004; Boe, Bobbit, & Cook, 1997; Fore, Martin, & Bender, 2002) are but three determinants contributing to the shortage of special education teachers.

Requests for reprints should be sent to Laurie U. deBettencourt, Northern Virginia Center, University of Virginia, 7054 Haycock Road, Falls Church, VA 22043. E-mail: debetten@virginia.edu

"Special education is facing the daunting challenge of increasing the supply of teachers while simultaneously upgrading its quality" (Brownell et al., 2002, p. 1). Data from the U.S. Department of Education suggested that in 1996–1997, more than 10% of special education teaching positions for children and youth between the ages 3 and 21 were either vacant or filled by teachers not fully certified (McIntire, 2001). Most of the school districts across the United States (98%) report special education teacher shortages (ERIC Clearinghouse on Disabilities and Gifted Education, 2001). According to the most recent data from the U.S. Department of Education (2003), "47,532 individuals filling special education positions (approximately 11.4% of all teachers) during the 2000–2001 school year lacked appropriate special education certification" (McLeskey et al., 2004, p. 7). Although shortages of special education personnel vary greatly by state (McLeskey et al., 2004), many of the increasing shortages have been evidenced in the areas of learning disabilities, emotional and behavioral disorders, mental retardation, and visual impairment (American Association for Employment in Education, 2000). The Bureau of Labor Statistics (2002–2003) projected employment of special education teachers to increase faster than the average for all occupations through 2010, spurred by continued growth in the number of special education students needing services, legislation emphasizing training and employment for individuals with disabilities, and educational reforms requiring higher standards for graduation. The Council for Exceptional Children (CEC) predicts that the United States will need more than 200,000 special education teachers to fill vacant positions by 2005 (Kozleski, Mainzer, Deshler, Coleman, & Rodriguez-Walling, 2000). Thus, an insufficient supply of new special education teachers, increasing special education student enrollments, and the high teacher attrition rates in special education have all contributed to a chronic national special education teacher shortage (Billingsley, 2004; McLeskey, Smith, Tyler, & Saunders, 2002).

In response to the national teacher shortages, alternative licensing routes have been supported by federal mandates (Billingsley & McLeskey, 2004; Brownell et al., 2002; Rosenberg & Sindelar, 2001). The Bush administration has developed policies to increase supply (e.g., the No Child Left Behind Act of 2001; Public Law 107–110; http://www.ed.gov/policy/elsec/leg/esea02/index.html) and promote relatively quick entry to the profession via alternative licensure routes. Alternative licensing routes, broadly defined as licensure programs not requiring traditional university teacher preparation, are increasing in number and variety (Feistritzer, 2000; Rosenberg & Sindelar, 2001; Wayman, Foster, Mantle-Bromley, & Wilson, 2003). In the United States, two thirds of teacher education institutions currently offer some type of alternative licensing routes (Barry, 2001). The current interest in alternative teacher licensure programs reflects not only teacher shortage concerns but also the concerns regarding traditional preparation of teachers and the commitment of individuals entering the teaching profession (Holmes, 2001; Kwiatkowski, 1999).

This push for alternative licensure programs, driven in part by the belief that traditional teacher education programs have failed to produce the highly qualified teachers that are needed (U.S. Department of Education, 2002), has encouraged federal funding initiatives. Because these initiatives promote quick entry into the profession they appear attractive to many outside the field of teaching. Several critics, however, dismiss alternative programs, especially those that remove certain requirements or lower standards for certification

(Billingsley & McLeskey, 2004). There are others, however, who believe alternative licensure routes are valuable in that they are crafted to meet the immediate needs of the school districts and attract career-changing professionals who stay involved in the field longer than many recent college graduates (Pipho, 2000). An encouraging feature of alternative licensure programs is the apparent success in recruiting (Feistritzer, 1994). It is believed that alternative licensure programs attract new groups of college graduates, particularly those from diverse backgrounds, to the profession (Pipho, 2000; Rosenberg & Rock, 1994; Zeichner & Schulte, 2001). Retention of new special education teachers is one area of concern. Kwiatkowski (1999) suggested many current young teachers do not see teaching as a long-term career. A small amount of existing research suggests that some of the alternative licensure programs may produce competent graduates who are likely to remain in teaching (Brownell et al., 2002; Zeichner & Schulte, 2001).

However, research findings on alternative licensure programs and retention are mixed. Some evidence suggests that alternatively licensed teachers have a lower attrition rate than traditionally trained teachers (Klagholz, 2000). Yet, others suggest the attrition rate of alternatively licensed teachers is nearly double the rate of attrition of traditionally trained teachers (Barry, 2001). Still other studies of alternative licensure programs have shown teachers trained in alternative licensure programs displayed lower skills in the area of instructional methods (Miller, McKenna, & McKenna, 1998). Some claim that alternatively licensed teachers have more difficulty learning to teach than do traditionally trained teachers (Barry, 2001).

If it is true that alternative programs are not adequately preparing teachers, these alternative programming solutions to the paucity of qualified teachers may actually exacerbate the problem by staffing classrooms of students most at risk of academic failure with teachers who may not have necessary content knowledge and skills that will help their students learn. Further, these alternatively licensed teachers may leave the profession more quickly because of their heightened concerns in the initial high-stress period (i.e., the first year of teaching). This lack of consensus suggests that all alternative licensure programs are not the same and that each type must be looked at distinctly.

Promising models of alternative licensure programs involve intensive, postbaccalaureate preparation to accommodate second-career professionals or noneducation majors (Brownell et al., 2002). These programs typically require (a) student participation in extensive coursework, (b) university faculty and experienced teachers' mentoring of teachers, and (c) collaboration between university faculty and school district personnel. Little research has examined the effectiveness of these components within alternative licensure training programs. Researchers should divert attention away from comparative studies and focus on gaining a better understanding of the components of good teacher education regardless of the structural model that is being studied. One method that may help make sense of the emerging and somewhat contradictory findings is to clearly describe the components of the alternative licensure program being studied so that the findings can be meaningfully placed within the context of the broader literature on similar programs.

The purpose of this article is to describe the components of one such federally funded initiative to alternatively license career changers in the area of special education and to provide insight into the participants' first-year reflections.

RECRUITING AND PREPARING OF SPECIAL EDUCATION
TEACHERS WITH SURVIVAL SKILLS

The Recruiting and Preparing of Special Education Teachers with Survival Skills (RAPSETSS), a federally funded project, recruited career-changing professionals with a minimum of a bachelor's degree and equipped them to become trained, confident, well-prepared special education teachers with an endorsement in learning disabilities. Each participant was given a job teaching special education within a public school. The program provided a university graduate school training in pedagogy and supervised teaching experiences. RAPSETSS met the state requirements for licensure in special education with an endorsement in learning disabilities. In addition, the three partners (i.e., the university faculty and programs, the public school district personnel, and the personnel of an education nonprofit organization) provided the participants with quality special education graduate school courses, immediate special education teaching positions, mentorship by experienced teachers, relevant resource materials, skill workshops, and constant guidance. The RAPSETSS model of alternative licensure involved intensive, postbaccalaureate preparation to accommodate second-career professionals with the goal of providing the field of special education with licensed teachers within two years.

As a whole the program's goals were threefold: (a) to address teacher shortages in the field of special education by identifying, hiring, and assisting career changers to become special education teachers with the challenges of teaching during the first two years (typically the most difficult years); (b) to help these beginning special educators develop the essential instructional skills, professional survival skills (e.g., time management, efficient paperwork processing), and self-confidence to remain in the field of special education as effective teachers; and (c) to facilitate their completion of the state's requirements for licensure in special education with an endorsement in learning disabilities within two years.

Each partner (i.e., university faculty and programs, nonprofit education personnel, and school district personnel) made unique contributions to the program, resulting in a richer preparation program for the participants. The university faculty offered the coursework, supervised field experiences, and career guidance needed to meet state licensure requirements to become effective special education teachers with an endorsement in learning disabilities. The course content paralleled that of the coursework offered in the traditional special education teacher education program at the same institution. The coursework preparation was provided at an accelerated pace on weekends and nights, enabling the participants to enter the teaching profession quickly (see Table 1 for a list of university coursework).

The nonprofit educational personnel and organization provided the participants with financial support (participants were given $1,000 each year to help pay for the cost of the coursework), counseling (i.e., a person with a doctorate trained in educational psychology and special education was available by phone and e-mail to talk about issues that developed), and professional materials (e.g., recent articles from professional journals) focused on topics relevant to beginning special education teachers. Specifically, the nonprofit organization, in cooperation with the university, developed

TABLE 1
University Coursework

Summer Year 1
 EDIS 511: Characteristics of People With Learning Disabilities (3 graduate credits)
 EDIS 589JE: Research Trends, Current Issues, and Legal Issues in Special Education (2 graduate credits)
Fall Year 1
 EDIS 705: Behavior Management (3 graduate credits)
Spring Year 1
 EDIS 508: Methods for Teaching Exceptional Children (3 graduate credits)
Summer Year 2
 EDIS 770: Foundations of Reading (3 graduate credits)
 EDIS 772: Word Study: Language Structures and Phonics (3 graduate credits)
 EDIS 589: Consultation (3 graduate credits)
Fall Year 2
 EDIS 504: Assessment Techniques for Exceptional Children (3 graduate credits)
Spring Year 2
 EDIS 589ME: Mathematics and Technology: Tools for the Special Educator (2 graduate credits)
 EDIS 789: Special Education Practicum (3 graduate credits)

---

and offered two summer institutes and several workshops. In addition, the nonprofit organization supported a discussion board on the Internet and a professor and counselor. The first institute was held during the first summer (prior to employment), and the second was held the summer after the first year of teaching. Each fall and spring additional workshops were offered on critical topic areas. All were customized to reflect the practical issues (e.g., paperwork) and concerns (e.g., behavior management) facing the participants during their first 2 years of teaching. The electronic discussion board and live counselor provided vehicles available at all times of the day for sharing common problems, solutions, and helpful hints. The nonprofit organization also provided many print resources (e.g., articles, books, and pamphlets) organized by topic (e.g., teaching of reading) on a regular basis.

The two school districts hired the participants and provided financial support (i.e., tuition for one course a year), first-year mentors, and typical school district resources (e.g., guidance from a department chairperson).

The participants applied to the university and were selected by the special education admissions committee in the late spring and early summer of 2002. During the summer the school districts interviewed the selected students and made final selections for specific classroom assignments. During the month of July the final list of participants enrolled in two graduate-level university courses (i.e., Characteristics of People With Learning Disabilities; Research Trends, Current Issues, and Legal Issues). In August, the teachers participated in workshops designed by the grant organizers and by their school district. During the fall, participants enrolled in one graduate-level university course on behavior management. In the spring, participants enrolled in one graduate-level university course on teaching methods. The fall and spring classes met on five Saturdays, and two additional workshops were held during one Friday night of each semester.

METHOD

Participants

Sixty-two individuals were accepted into the RAPSETSS program; however, during the first 2 months of the first school year, 3 left the program for family or health reasons, leaving a total of 59 participants. There were 14 (24%) men and 45 (76%) women. Their ages ranged from 21 to 64 years of age. The largest age group was 21 to 29 years with 20 participants (34%). There were 6 participants with ages of 30 to 39 years (10%), and 16 participants with ages between 40 and 49 years (27%). In addition, there were 15 participants with ages between 50 and 59 years (26%), and 2 participants with ages over 60 years (3%). There were 6 African Americans (10%), 3 Asian Americans (5%), 48 Caucasians (81%), and 2 "other" participants (3%). Although at the time of selection no one was teaching elementary or secondary students, over half of the participants' occupations were in the field of education, with many serving as instructional assistants (see Table 2 for participant information).

Schools

The two partner school districts participating in this collaborative project were located in a southeastern state. School District A, one of the 100 largest suburban school districts in the United States, had an enrollment of 265,920, with 8% served in special education (Virginia Department of Education, 2001). In 2001, there were 198 schools and 12,310 teachers. The school district had a mean household income of $92,146, with less than 4% of households at or below the poverty level (U.S. Census, 2000). The 47 participants in School District A were placed into teaching positions in 34 different schools at the elementary, middle, and secondary level.

School District B, one of the 500 largest suburban school districts in the United States, had a student enrollment of 46,444 (U.S. Census, 2000), with 8% served in special education (Virginia Department of Education, 2001). As of 2003, there were 61 schools and 3,356 teachers. School District B had a mean household income of $88,387, with less than 3% of households at or below the poverty level (U.S. Census, 2000). Twelve participants were placed in 12 different schools at the elementary, middle, and secondary level.

Materials

The three surveys consisted of two parts. The first part consisted of nine Likert-type questions, with answers on scales ranging from 1 (*strongly disagree*) to 4 (*strongly agree*), regarding participants' attitudes toward their teaching experiences. Not all nine questions were asked each time (see Table 3 for list of questions). The second part consisted of six open-ended questions concerning their teaching experiences. The first three open-ended questions asked participants why they chose special education as a career, how they judged their teaching performance, and how they described a bad teacher. The third open-ended question asking participants to describe a bad teacher was deleted after the fall survey. The fall and spring surveys included two additional open-ended questions

TABLE 2
Participants

Characteristic	n	%
Gender		
Male	14	24
Female	45	76
Age (in years)		
20–29	20	34
30–39	6	10
40–49	16	27
50–59	15	26
≥60	2	3
Race[a]		
Caucasian	48	81
Asian	3	5
African American	6	10
Other	2	3
Prior occupation[a]		
Education	35	59
Instructional assistant	22	37
Substitute	10	17
Interpreter	1	2
Athletic trainer	1	2
Educational coordinator	1	2
Noneducation	24	41
Law	1	1
Nursing	2	3
Clerical	4	7
Management	10	17
Food service	3	5
Babysitting	1	2
Real estate	1	2
Government	1	2
Sales	1	2

Note. $N = 59$.
[a]Percentages do not total 100 due to rounding.

TABLE 3
Likert-Type Questions

1. I feel confident in my ability to teach [Not asked in fall]
2. I often feel disorganized in my classroom
3. Teaching is harder than I expected [Not asked in summer]
4. I feel every day that I become a better teacher
5. I find the other teachers at my school to be helpful
6. I telephone, e-mail, or talk with other special education teachers to share ideas and gain support [Not asked in summer]
7. My mentor has helped me with lesson planning, time management, or discipline
8. In 5 years, I will be teaching special education
9. I have read or used resource materials in special education

related to their mentoring experiences. In the spring and the summer two open-ended questions were added related to the teachers' views of the RAPSETSS program and their specific teaching classroom assignment. There was also one open-ended question about their school's emergency preparedness added to the spring survey.

Procedure

The surveys were distributed three times during the participants' first year of teaching. The first survey was distributed at the fall (October) workshop with a stamped addressed envelope to assist participants in returning them. The second survey was mailed to all participants with instructions to complete and return when they attended the spring (April) workshop. The third survey was distributed and completed during the summer (August) workshop after their first year of teaching.

RESULTS

There were 33 of 59 fall surveys returned, for a return rate of 56%. There were 46 of 59 spring surveys returned, for a return rate of 78%. There were 43 of 59 summer surveys returned, for a return rate of 73%. The results are discussed in terms of the participants' view of their teaching, mentoring, and professional development experiences.

Teaching Experiences

Similar to teachers prepared through traditional routes to licensure, project participants increased their confidence in their ability to teach as the academic year progressed. Eighty-seven percent (40 of 46) of the participants felt confident in their ability to teach in spring, and 98% (42 of 43) felt confident by the summer. Sixty-six percent (22 of 33) of the respondents felt teaching was harder than expected in the fall, and 63% (29 of 46) felt that way in the spring. Eighty percent (29 of 33) felt they had become better teachers as time passed in the fall, and 98% (45 of 46) felt they had improved by the spring. All (43 of 43) felt they had improved by the summer. Many teachers during their first year feel disorganized, and these participants were no different. Sixty percent (20 of 33) of the teachers felt disorganized in their classroom in the fall, 37% (17 of 46) in the spring, and 81% (35 of 43) in the summer. Most teachers felt other teachers in their school were helpful. All but 3 on each survey found other teachers to be helpful. Seventy-three percent (24 of 33) shared ideas with other teachers in the fall, and 80% (37 of 46) did so in the spring (see Table 4).

In the fall when participants answered the open-ended questions relating to their teaching experiences, 30% (10 of 33) responded that they were surprised by the low academic functioning levels of their students. Twelve percent (4 of 33) commented on how tired they were at the end of the day. Fifteen percent (5 of 33) of the participants were surprised by the amount and detail of individualized education program (IEP) paperwork, and 3% (1 of 33) were surprised at how demanding the parents of the students were. Fifteen percent (5 of 33) of the participants were surprised by negative interactions with other teachers or felt a lack of support from other teachers. One participant commented that she was surprised at how much she enjoyed teaching.

TABLE 4
Responses

Statements	Term	Respondents N	SD n	SD %	D n	D %	A n	A %	SA n	SA %
1. I feel confident in my	Fall	NA	—	—	—	—	—	—	—	—
ability to teach	Spring	46	0	0	6	13	25	54	15	33
	Summer	43	1	2	0	0	29	67	13	30
2. I often feel	Fall	33	1	3	12	36	18	55	2	6
disorganized in my	Spring	46	5	11	24	52	12	26	5	11
classroom	Summer	43	2	4	6	14	25	58	10	23
3. Teaching is harder	Fall	33	2	6	9	27	12	36	10	30
than I expected	Spring	46	4	8	13	28	16	35	13	28
	Summer	NA	—	—	—	—	—	—	—	—
4. I feel every day that I	Fall	33	1	3	3	9	18	54	11	33
become a better	Spring	46	0	0	1	2	21	46	24	52
teacher	Summer	43	0	0	0	0	21	48	22	51
5. I find the other	Fall	33	0	0	3	9	11	33	19	58
teachers at my school	Spring	46	0	0	3	7	28	61	15	33
to be helpful	Summer	43	0	0	3	6	24	56	16	37
6. I telephone, e-mail, or	Fall	33	1	3	8	24	18	55	6	18
talk with other special	Spring	46	3	7	6	13	24	52	13	28
education teachers ...	Summer	NA	—	—	—	—	—	—	—	—
7. My mentor has helped	Fall	33	7	21	9	27	6	18	11	33
me with lesson	Spring	46	3	7	13	28	14	30	16	35
planning ...	Summer	43	5	12	9	21	14	33	15	35
8. In 5 years, I will be	Fall	33	4	12	4	12	10	30	15	45
teaching special	Spring	46	2	4	5	11	24	52	15	33
education	Summer	43	6	14	4	9	22	51	11	33
9. I have read or used	Fall	33	6	13	16	48	9	27	2	6
resource materials in	Spring	46	0	0	8	17	30	65	8	17
special education	Summer	43	0	0	3	6	27	63	13	30

Note.   SD = strongly disagree; D = disagree; A = agree; SA = strongly agree; NA = not asked.

In the fall, 36% (12 of 33) stated the most important thing they had learned in the first 6 weeks was the importance of realistic expectations, including how to be flexible and consistent. Another 24% (8 of 33) stated the most important things they had learned were how to (a) communicate, (b) prioritize, and (c) organize paperwork.

The final open-ended question of the fall survey provided an opportunity for respondents to communicate other areas of concern or interest. Several of the respondents commented on how grateful or thankful they were to the RAPSETSS program. Several respondents commented on the difficulty of workshops and general feelings of fatigue.

On the spring survey's open-ended questions, 30% (14 of 46) of the participants stated that the things they wished they had known at the beginning of the year were lesson planning or methods of instruction. Specifically, 17% (8 of 46) of the participants discussed the paperwork and IEP requirements as things they felt overwhelmed by and wished they had known about at the beginning of the school year. An additional 13% (6 of 46) of the participants wished they had had better behavior and classroom management skills.

On the summer survey open-ended questions, 30% (13 of 43) stated that the things they wished they had known at the beginning of the year were lesson planning and methods of instruction. An additional 21% (9 of 43) of the participants wished they had better classroom management skills. An additional 26% (12 of 43) of the teachers commented that teaching was harder than they expected, the cost of the courses was more than expected, and they lacked knowledge of available resources within their school system.

At the end of their first year the open-ended comments included 51% (22 of 43) of the participants stating that they were surprised by how positive their teaching experience their first year had been. Fourteen percent (6 of 43) reported being surprised that teaching was harder than expected, and an additional 9% (4 of 43) of participants were surprised by the behavior of their students. Twelve percent (5 of 43) of participants mentioned that team teaching and collaboration with general education teachers was harder than expected.

In the fall, 75% (25 of 33) felt they would be teaching special education in 5 years. Eighty-five percent (39 of 46) in the spring and 77% (33 of 43) in the summer felt they would be teaching special education in 5 years.

Mentoring Experiences

For many first-year teachers the mentoring experience is seen as very helpful. For this group of beginning teachers the positive mentoring experiences increased as the year progressed. Fifty-one percent (17 of 33) in the fall felt their mentors were helpful. In the spring, 65% (30 of 46) believed their mentors were helpful. In the summer, 67% (29 of 43) believed their mentors were helpful.

The spring and summer survey contained questions about experiences with their mentor. On the spring survey, 52% (24 of 46) of the participants discussed positive experiences with their mentors. An additional 37% (17 of 46) of the participants expressed that they had excellent mentors. Eleven percent (5 of 46) of the participants expressed negative experiences with their mentors, including 2 participants who stated that they disliked and distrusted their mentors. On the summer survey, 21% (9 of 43) expressed that they would have liked more time with their mentor or additional help from their mentor. Sixteen percent (7 of 43) of the participants reported negative interactions with their mentors. Two (4%) did not respond to this question.

Professional Development Experiences

The first year of teaching for this group was spent taking five graduate courses, and thus their professional development was intense. Many felt they had little time to participate in any additional professional development. By the spring of their first year, only 18 teachers of the participants who completed the surveys (39%) had joined a professional organization. Thirteen of the 18 joined their local education association or union, with 5 additionally joining a special education professional organization (i.e., the CEC), and 4 of the 18 participants reported also joining the National Education Association. Two of the 18 reported additionally joining another professional organization but had forgotten the name. This question was also asked on the summer survey at the end of their first year, and over half (23 of 43) had not joined a professional organization.

In the fall, many of the teachers (16 of 33, or 48%) did not read or use resources. In the spring, over three fourths (38 of 46, or 83%) did, and in the summer almost all (40 of 43, or 93%) respondents were reading and using other resources.

DISCUSSION

Given that the supply of graduates from traditional teacher education programs is inadequate to meet the demand for new teachers and that burgeoning shortages loom on the horizon, alternative routes to licensure represent a viable strategy for increasing the supply (Brownell et al., 2002). However, alternative routes to licensure encompass a wide range of programs, and research needs to continue to describe and review the components of such programs.

The RAPSETSS program was an example of an intensive training program with parameters guided by federal and state restrictions, and the individuals were placed in special education teaching positions after completing only two graduate-level education training courses. The federal directives required that the participants be put into classrooms during the first year of the grant. In addition, given that there was only 1 month for training and the state requirements for a conditional license mandated that we cover legal issues and characteristics of exceptional students in our preteaching preparation, we were limited in the coverage of methods or behavior management issues. This lack of instructional methods or behavior management courses until after the individuals were teaching in their own classrooms was reflected in the participants' feeling of surprise at the lack of academic and behavior skills of the students they taught. Their feelings of inadequacy in the areas of behavior management and teaching methods were further reflected in their open-ended comments that they would have liked to have more knowledge of the curriculum and appropriate teaching methods.

Many of these new teachers commented in their first fall that teaching was much harder than they expected. Many stated they were physically and emotionally exhausted. In addition, it should be noted that in October of their first year, the greater Washington, DC, suburbs were affected by sniper shootings. Many of the schools were in "lockdown," and many extracurricular and outdoor activities, including recess, were canceled or held inside for the 22 days of the shootings. Although any teacher would have had difficulty under these conditions, the participants in the RAPSETSS program were new to the profession, and this complicated their adjustment to the school environment.

Yet, by spring most of the participants felt confident in their teaching ability and by summer almost all were confident. In addition, most felt they were getting better every day in their teaching. Most used other teachers for help and believed their mentors were helpful. Many who responded to the mentoring questions on the survey were pleased with their mentors. Yet, many did not respond to questions directed at their mentoring experiences. We do not know if the nonresponders were not as pleased. As a result of their lack of response and our limited knowledge (i.e., anecdotal information given to the counselors of the grant), we have added more avenues to collect information on the mentoring piece of the new teacher puzzle. We believe that good mentoring is critical for new career-changing teachers. Most school districts provide mentors for first-year teachers, and both school districts here did as well. However, the mentors were not always in the same field. It might be good to provide new special education teachers with seasoned special education mentors.

During the first fall of their teaching experience few teachers found time to use resources or outside materials beyond the graduate classes they were obligated to take. By the spring and the summer more of the teachers were finding time for outside resources. Yet, the lack of professional development opportunities chosen by these new teachers may reflect a lack of understanding of the need to be part of the larger teaching profession or just a lack of time. It is not clear these new teachers understood what they would gain from joining such teaching organizations as the CEC and the National Education Association. In addition, it may have been too much to ask of many of them, as they were spending most of their time trying to be prepared for each day of teaching, to expect them to look at the bigger picture of teachers' professional advocacy organizations. We have added more awareness sessions in which opportunities will exist to explain to the group the goals and purposes of several professional teaching organizations.

Limitations

There are several limitations to this study. The return rate for our surveys was not 100%, and thus we will never know what the nonresponders felt about their teaching. We do know more from the phone calls and questions asked at the workshops, but these data are not included in this article. We also did not ask every question on every survey, so the change over time was not available with each question. We believe from talking to the teachers and others in the area that the 3 weeks of sniper activity in the Washington, DC, area had an effect on all teachers. We also had staff changes within the nonprofit education organization, and the individual closest to the teachers, who acted as a counselor to them, changed after the first 3 months. The teachers did discuss the departure of this individual.

Future Alternative Licensure Programs

When this opportunity to make a career change to teaching in the field of special education was advertised, it was set up to attract older career changers, yet our largest group of applicants accepted into the program was within the 20 to 29 age range. Many of the individuals within this age range were instructional assistants recommended by their school district to apply to our grant. The individuals within this group seemed generally more positive and seemed to make the transition easier (as noted in telephone conversations with the counselor). It may make sense to develop alternative licensure programs for individuals who are knowledgeable of the current school milieu and may need financial and instructional assistance to make the transition into the classroom as a teacher.

The participants in one school district were part of a large cohort (49 participants). They took classes together, came to workshops together, and some taught at the same schools. The cohort concept helped many of them find emotional support. Yet, several negative aspects of the cohort mechanism were noticed as the year progressed. Many more reserved participants looked for advice from the more outspoken cohort members, and the outspoken participants who offered the advice were not always the best teachers or the best students. Several "leaders" presented strong negative attitudes toward teaching and the personnel attempting to help within their schools. The second school district cohort (10 participants) took courses during the school year with other more experienced teachers. These new teachers stated they learned a great deal from the other more experienced teachers in their classes. Teaching groups by using a cohort model may need to be mixed with experienced teachers seeking professional development. It may prove helpful to have more experienced teachers who are taking courses either as part of a master's degree or professional development to mix with the new career changers.

CONCLUSIONS

We do not know if the alternative training program described in this article prepared these teachers to teach special education students well. We do know that all 59 continued into their second year of teaching. Most appeared to be feeling positive and confident about their teaching experiences as they entered their second year. Yet, this second year will prove crucial, as the participants need to pass the state Praxis I licensing exam (Praxis I includes items on basic math, reading, and writing) and also be retained by their school districts. We will not know for a few years if these alternatively licensed teachers will leave the profession more quickly because of their heightened concerns and stresses in the initial two-year period. We do believe that the education coursework and training they received was critical, along with the much-needed emotional and mentoring support. As all alternative licensure programs are not the same, we must begin to document what pieces work and how they work.

REFERENCES

American Association for Employment in Education. (2000). *Educator supply and demand.* Columbus, OH: Author.

Barry, B. (2001). No shortcuts to preparing good teachers. *Educational Leadership, 58*(8), 32–36.

Billingsley, B. S. (2004). Special education teacher retention and attrition: A critical analysis of the research literature. *Journal of Special Education, 38,* 39–55.

Billingsley, B. S., & McLeskey, J. (2004). Critical issues in special education teacher supply and demand: Overview. *Journal of Special Education, 38,* 2–4.

Boe, E., Bobbit, S. A., & Cook, L. H. (1997). Whither didst thou go? Retention, reassignment, migration, and attrition of special and general education teachers from a national perspective. *Journal of Special Education, 30,* 371–389.

Brownell, M. T., Sindelar, P. T., Bishop, A. G., Langley, L. K., & Seo, S. (2002). Special education teacher supply and teacher quality: The problems, the solutions. *Focus on Exceptional Children, 35*(2), 1–16.

Bureau of Labor Statistics. (2002–2003). *Occupational outlook handbook 2002–2003 edition*. Retrieved January 16, 2004, from http://www.bls.gov/oco/ocos070.htm

Elementary and Secondary Education Act. (2001). *No Child Left Behind Act of 2001*. Washington, DC: U.S. Department of Education. Retrieved November 23, 2004, from http://www.ed.gov/policy/elsec/leg/esea02/index.html

ERIC Clearinghouse on Disabilities and Gifted Education. (2001, April). *Educating exceptional children: A statistical profile*. Arlington, VA: Council for Exceptional Children.

Feistritzer, E. (1994). The evolution of alternative teacher certification. *The Educational Forum, 6,* 132–138.

Feistritzer, E. (2000). *Alternative teacher licensure*. Washington, DC: National Center for Education Information.

Fore, C., III, Martin, C., & Bender, W. N. (2002). Teacher burnout in special education: The causes and the recommended solutions. *High School Journal, 86*(1), 36–44.

Holmes, B. J. (2001). Understanding the pros and cons of alternative routes to teacher certification. *Teaching and Change, 8,* 317–330.

Klagholz, L. (2000, January). *Growing better teachers in the garden state: New Jersey's "alternative route" to teacher certification*. Washington, DC: Thomas Fordham Foundation.

Kozleski, E., Mainzer, R. W., Deshler, D., Coleman, M. R., & Rodriguez-Walling, M. (2000). *Bright futures for exceptional learners: An agenda to achieve quality conditions for teaching and learning*. Arlington, VA: Council for Exceptional Children.

Kwiatkowski, M. (1999). *Debating alternative teaching certification: A trail by achievement*. Washington, DC: Thomas Fordham Foundation. Retrieved January 15, 2003, from http://www.edexcellence.net/foundation/publication/publication.cfm?id=15#50

McIntire, J. (2001, July 13). Market forces and special education. *Education Week, 20*(40), 37.

McLeskey, J., Smith, D. D., Tyler, N., & Saunders, S. (2002). *The supply and demand for special education teachers: A review of research regarding the nature of the chronic shortage of special education*. Gainesville, FL: Center on Personnel Studies in Special Education.

McLeskey, J., Tyler, N. C., & Flippin, S. S. (2004). The supply of and demand for special education teachers: A review of research regarding the chronic shortage of special education teachers. *Journal of Special Education, 38,* 5–21.

Miller, J. W., McKenna, M. C., & McKenna, B. A. (1998). A comparison of alternatively and traditionally prepared teachers. *Journal of Teacher Education, 49,* 165–176.

Pipho, C. (1998). A real teacher shortage. *Phi Delta Kappan, 80,* 181.

Pipho, C. (2000). Stateline—A new reform model of teachers and teaching. *Phi Delta Kappan, 81,* 421.

Rosenberg, M. S., & Rock, E. E. (1994). Alternative certification in special education: Efficacy of a collaborative, field-based teacher preparation program. *Teacher Education and Special Education, 17,* 141–153.

Rosenberg, M. S., & Sindelar, P. T. (2001). *The proliferation of alternative routes to certification in special education: A critical review of the literature*. Arlington, VA: National Clearing House for Professions in Special Education, Council for Exceptional Children.

U.S. Census. (2000). *Income*. Retrieved December 13, 2003, from http://www.census.gov/hhes/wwww/income/html

U.S. Department of Education. (2001). *Twenty-third annual report to Congress on the implementation of the Individuals with Disabilities Education Act*. Washington, DC: Author.

U.S. Department of Education. (2002). *Meeting the highly qualified teachers challenge: The Secretary's annual report on teacher quality*. Washington, DC: U.S. Department of Education, Office of Postsecondary Education.

U.S. Department of Education. (2003). *Individuals with Disabilities Education Act (IDEA) data*. Retrieved from http://www.ideadata.org

Virginia Department of Education. (2001). *Special education report*. Retrieved December 13, 2003, from http://www.pen.k12.va.us/VDOE/Publications

Wayman, J. C., Foster, A. M., Mantle-Bromley, C., & Wilson, C. (2003). A comparison of the professional concerns of traditionally prepared and alternatively licensed new teachers. *High School Journal, 86*(3), 35–40.

Zeichner, K. M., & Schulte, A. K. (2001). What we know and don't know from peer-reviewed research about alternative teacher certification programs. *Journal of Teacher Education, 52,* 266–282.

EXCEPTIONALITY, *12*(4), 239–246

Reflections on 20 Years of Preparing Special Education Teachers

Anne M. Bauer, Lawrence J. Johnson, and Regina H. Sapona
College of Education, Criminal Justice, and Human Services
University of Cincinnati

The preparation of special educators has changed dramatically since the Individuals with Disabilities Education Act was implemented. Special education teachers must deal with changes in the political contexts in which they work as well as changes in the children, youth, and families with whom they work. As a consequence of those changes, how we prepare teachers has become much more complex. Teacher education programs are being asked to demonstrate how their candidates impact children's achievement in ways that we have never had to before. Although the need for research-based approaches is as critical as it was 20 years ago, the quality of research on teacher education has improved. The stakes are much higher: Unless we incorporate research-based practices into our programs and use that research to improve our preparation programs, alternative pathways to licensure and certification may become the norm.

As faculty members who began our careers in the 1980s, we once discussed our "special education family trees." This discussion was essentially about evolution—what we were taught, and what we taught. For our mentors, special education was a new revolution, fighting for the educability of all children. As we began our careers as teacher educators, we were excited by the opportunity to guide the preparation of both special and general education teachers as they developed skills, dispositions, and a commitment to meeting the needs of all children. Yet, the Individuals with Disabilities Education Act (IDEA) is more than 25 years old and had a difficult time in reauthorization. "No Child Left Behind" is edging in on our territory. We are spending large amounts of time rationalizing our practice with assessment systems for accreditation. Unfortunately, we have come under serious fire by policymakers, and our teacher education programs are in serious question. As special educators we are used to adapting; the speed of adaptation, however, is making it difficult for us to reflect on our work as teacher educators. Yet, we are confronted with three strands of changes: changes in educator preparation; changes in the political context in which we work; and changes in the children, youth, and families who are our ultimate consumers.

Requests for reprints should be sent to Anne M. Bauer, Division of Teacher Education, University of Cincinnati, P.O. Box 210002, Cincinnati, OH 45221. E-mail: anne.bauer@uc.edu

CHANGES IN EDUCATOR PREPARATION

In her analysis of the "outcomes question" in teacher education, Cochran-Smith (2000) described a loose chronology. During the 1950s and 1960s, researchers sought to describe the attributes and qualities of good teaching. In the 1980s and 1990s, knowledge questions emerged, with efforts to identify what educators should know. Currently, questions of outcome require that teachers show us what they can do, describing professional performance as outcomes. Because special education was such a new thing in the 1960s, we were a bit behind in this chronology. With the new Council for Exceptional Children (CEC, 2003) standards, however, we must demonstrate that our students—"candidates" in the parlance of accreditation—can indeed perform.

Special educators, however, do not perform in a vacuum. There is a societal context to the work of all teachers, which perhaps, has even greater impact for special educators. Almost two decades ago Britzman (1986) described three myths that were part of the societal context for teachers. First, there was the myth that everything that happens in the classroom depends on the educator. The educator was somehow in control and was able to instill knowledge. Second, educators were experts, and that which they profess (usually in the form of textbooks or institutionalized materials) was the truth. The third myth was even more challenging. It suggests that educators were self-made from experience rather than from their professional preparation. These three myths are still evident in the context of special education teacher preparation.

In 1996 past recipients of the Teacher Education Division award for the outstanding publication of the year were asked to reflect on the past 20 years of special education (Spooner & Johnson, 1996). Rosenburg (1996) suggested that as a field, we have made significant progress in understanding how to best educate students with disabilities. Unfortunately, our teacher education programs have not uniformly kept pace with this knowledge base. He further asserted: "In my view, it is this irony that underlies much of what needs to be addressed in teacher education and special" (p. 209). Greenwood (2001) was a topical editor an issue of *Teacher Education and Special Education* focusing on the gap between research and practice. A review of these articles clearly indicates that the gap between research and practice described by Rosenburg still exists (Sindelar & Brownell, 2001). Although we are energized by the emerging research on teacher education, it is clear that we must do a better job of incorporating research-based practice into our teacher education programs (The Teaching Commission, 2004).

Without question, we must fully embrace a research-based foundation for our practice. Otherwise, trial-and-error learning during field experiences will continue as a common way of learning the profession. From this perspective, people believe that the best way to learn is by experience. However, if practices are not grounded in research and theory, this experience generally reinforces the candidates' concept of practice they already have before entering their professional preparation program. When research and theory are devalued and practice glorified, the preparation of teachers becomes a vocational rather than a professional endeavor. As Johnson (2002) asserted in his testimony to the U.S. House of Representatives Committee on the status of teacher education, "doing teacher education right is hard work" (p. 1), and we must stop chasing magic bullets and get down to the hard work of educating teachers. He went on to suggest that the research is clear on what is needed: (a) strong content preparation, (b) research-based practices, and (c) heavily mentored practical experiences. Brownell, Ross, Colon, and McCallum (2003) described seven features of effective programs:

- Coherent, shared vision.
- Conscious effort to blend theory, content knowledge, and pedagogical knowledge from research with practice.
- Carefully designed field experiences.
- Standards based.
- Pedagogy that is active and research based.
- An emphasis on meeting the needs of a diverse population of students.
- Collaboration for building the professional community.

The tensions between theory and practice—the disconnection our students feel about their content area and education courses—are a challenge to our preparing special educators. Connelly and Clandinin (1988) suggested utilizing McKeon's (1952) description of the perspectives of this tenuous relation. The logistic perspective of the theory–practice relation argues that practice is applied theory and that developing theory is independent of practice. In McKeon's operational relation, practitioners are the source of the problems studied by researchers. This is the world of needs assessments, in which practitioners are manipulated or persuaded to participate in prescriptive interventions and programs to fix the problems of their efforts. In the third perspective, the problematic view, the professional is reflective and sees practice as a sequence of problem-solving episodes. Theory is not essential, and solutions to problems are local rather than general and theoretical. In the dialectic view, theory and practice are inseparable—practice is theory in action. As Connelly and Clandinin suggested: "The dialectic inquirer, both the practitioner in the school and the researcher in the university, government, or board of education, no longer watches situations, but rather participates in them" (p. 95).

This perception of theory and practice in constant conversation presents challenges. Our candidates bring with them a conception of the professional's tasks, and part of our role is deconstructing these conceptions. For example, candidates may view educators as guides, friends, or confidantes in the image of their favorite teacher rather than as professionals engaged in finding new meanings of teaching and learning (Calderhead, 1996). We recognize that schools may be engaged in the "fix it" model of special education. That is, new practices and structures may be handed down to educators without giving consideration to the ways they understand learning, ignoring the knowledge base educators bring to their work, and forcing them to use prescriptive materials that deny their continuous development of constructions about teaching and learning (Gitlin, 1990).

As a profession, we have made progress, and although there are still critical problems and challenges for us to address, the status of teacher education and special education has greatly improved. The National Council on Accreditation for Teacher Education (NCATE) standards and Praxis testing have increased the emphasis on content knowledge. We have rigorous, national, performance-based standards that define the expectations of the knowledge and skills of special educators that have significantly impacted our teacher education programs (Otis-Wilborn & Winn, 2000). Our professional standards (CEC) have forced us to align with the Interstate New Teacher Assessment and Support Consortium (INTASC) standards, and we have become more concerned about demonstrating that our candidates can perform and have an impact on children's learning. We are spending a great deal of time assessing what we do and designing appropriate assessment systems. This focus on accountability is long overdue and critical if teacher education is to survive. Our profession is under serious attack, and some have called for the dismantling of the current system of teacher education.

CHANGES IN THE POLITICAL CONTEXT

In July 2002, the President's Commission on Excellence in Special Education published *A New Era: Revitalizing Special Education for Children and Their Families* (U.S. Department of Education, Office of Special Education and Rehabilitative Services, 2002). This report issued several recommendations that were not earth shattering. No one would argue that we should recruit and train highly qualified general and special educators or create research- and data-driven educator preparation programs. Yet, some of their statements should make us very nervous. For example:

- "Teacher preparation institutions must move from folk wisdom, weak research and opinion on what are important characteristics of effective teachers and begin to focus on helping to strengthen the teacher competencies that have clear data for producing student gains" (p. 57).
- "We find no direct relationship between increased results for children with disabilities and whether a teacher holds a certificate or license" (p. 56).

As we have previously argued, we have rigorous, national, performance-based standards, yet the authors of the report apparently feel we make up our programs as we go along. In addition, the products of our efforts—teachers with certificates or licenses—are not held in esteem. This political context has furthered the drive for alternative pathways to the teaching profession. That is, if we do not know what we are doing, and if what we are doing makes no difference, are not alternative pathways just as good (and cheaper)? This embracing of alternative pathways is grounded in a vocational view of special education in which experience is emphasized and theory- and research-based practices are deemphasized. It is also ironic that calls for alternative pathways come at the same time that there are frantic calls for raising the quality of teacher education by increasing professional standards and recruiting the most talented into teaching (The Teaching Commission, 2004). Moreover, many of the alternative pathways are designed to replace the bureaucratic red tape of teacher education programs, which were put in place by the same policymakers that are promoting alternative pathways.

At this point, the vast majority of states have an alternative pathway to become a teacher. Alternative pathways vary by state and are designed to achieve different goals and objectives. Studies that compare traditional and alternative certification routes have yielded inconclusive results. Unfortunately, some data suggest that recipients of teaching credentials through alternative pathways end up in the most challenging school situations (National Center for Alternative Certification, 2004). It is also clear that the recruitment, preparation, and retention of teachers is much more complex than policymakers are willing to admit, and it is doubtful that these alternative pathways will be the solution to teacher quality or even teacher shortages. Without question we need more data on the effectiveness of alternative pathways, and we need greater emphasis on establishing the accountability and impact of our teacher education programs.

Increased accountability of our special education teacher preparation programs has changed our work. Similar to the reporting requirements of K–12 schools to prepare report cards on the achievement of their students, for the past several years, higher education institutions must report on the quality of teacher education graduates. Just as K–12 teachers spend weeks preparing students for proficiency tests, our teacher education programs focus on preparing our preservice teachers for certification or licensure tests. This practice can be helpful, and these data are important to helping us improve our practice and establish program impact. Unfortunately, policymakers have used this type of data as a stick to encourage improved practice. That is, data are used to characterize and compare programs, and little emphasis is placed on having these data be a part of a continuous improvement system. For example, public schools that have students who do not perform well may be placed on "academic watch" or "academic emergency." Title II reporting (U.S. Department of Education, National Center for Education Statistics, 2000) requires each state to develop a report card for its teacher education programs, and now teacher education programs have classifications such as "low performing" or "conditional approval" that are based on candidate performance on standardized tests and sometimes on graduate performance once they are teaching. We are not opposed to these data systems; however, we strongly believe that there needs to be greater emphasis on proactive ways to encourage continuous improvement as opposed to the development of labels designed to embarrass low-performing programs. Although the public has a right to know about the performance of teacher education programs, a continuous improvement orientation has the greatest potential to help us produce better teachers.

CHANGES IN THE CHILDREN, YOUTH, AND FAMILIES WE SERVE

Special education teachers today face dramatic changes in the students served in our schools and communities. Our classrooms, particularly in urban settings, include more diverse learners. When we first began as teachers in special education, we were sensitive to the impact cultural diversity might have on the assessments we used to identify learners who have special needs. We are now horrified when we think back to what was referred to as "environmental, cultural, or economic disadvantage," which was a part of the exclusionary clause in the federal definition of learning disabilities. Our communities are more economically diverse as well as culturally diverse now, and we must prepare our future special education teachers to address that diversity.

As the diversity in our classrooms, schools, and communities increases, our personnel preparation programs necessarily have changed. In contrast to the one course on diversity in a personnel preparation program, our courses are now infused with content knowledge and skills about culturally and linguistically diverse learners. Our field experiences should include multiple and varied experiences with diverse learners. Just as years ago a single course or two on "mainstreaming" was the norm in the preparation of general education teachers, now personnel preparation programs must provide content coursework and experiences that will help teachers organize classroom learning environments and instruction designed to meet the needs of all learners.

As with general education preparation programs, we too face the challenge of recruiting and retaining diverse teachers. In their review of recruitment and retention strategies for diverse teachers, Patton, Williams, Floyd, and Cobb (2003) described critical features of successful programs: setting goals and objectives for recruitment, providing programs to sensitize faculty to diversity and issues that affect minority students, the use of peer support in the form of cohorts, and providing academic support and flexibility in the programs of study. They revealed that early field experiences, strong collaborative efforts with public schools, orientation programs to help students adjust to campus life, and efforts to recruit and attract minority faculty were also factors of successful programs. They also noted the benefits of connecting to teacher academies at the high school level. The challenge of meeting the needs of diverse learners and addressing the complex needs of families comes at the same time we are pressured to provide our candidates with flexible programs and content knowledge to pass licensure tests.

CONCLUSIONS

We began this article thinking about adapting to the rapid changes in our work as teacher educators. Severe shortages in the number of special educators needed to fill positions in our schools has put great pressure on teacher educators to provide flexible preparation programs and do a better job of recruiting diverse teachers.

Previously we mentioned a 1996 topical issue of *Teacher Education and Special Education* in which past recipients of the Teacher Education Division's award for the outstanding publication of the year were asked to reflect on the past 20 years of special education. In that issue, Johnson (1996) asserted:

> After a great deal of reflection, it seems to me that our most pressing future challenge is the same challenge that faced us in the mid 70s, that is how do we define ourselves and how do we fit into a broader, educational, social, and economic context. (p. 204)

After completing this exercise we have had a similar reaction. We continue to grow as a field, and teacher education programs are vastly superior to those of 20 years ago. However, we have not come far enough, and it is critical that we go further. Twenty years ago there was a need for a more research-based approach, and the gap between research and practice was too wide. Although the gap has been closing, the same assertion can be made today. There are two significant differences between the past and now. First, the stakes are much higher today than they were in the past. Policymakers and other critics are seriously attacking our profession. Some have even suggested that we should dismantle teacher education programs and create alternative pathways that do not involve teacher education departments or colleges. If critics get their way, alternative pathways will become the main pathway to teaching. Our leisurely pace of incorporating research into our practice has contributed to this risky political challenge, and we must close this gap with great haste. Fortunately, the second thing that is different now from the past is the quality of research on teacher education. The research on teacher education has greatly improved in the last decade. For example, we have been involved with the Ohio Partnership for Accountability (2003), which is a comprehensive longitudinal study that involves essentially all of the teacher education programs in Ohio. In this study, components of teacher education programs are being quantified, and a path model is being created that will quantify the importance of teacher education components on student achievement. We must expeditiously incorporate research-based practices into teacher education and use the research on teacher education to improve our programs. Given the political context, moving at our leisurely pace of the past will mean the current alternative pathways will become the norm.

REFERENCES

Britzman, D. P. (1986). Cultural myths in the making of a teacher: Biography and social structure in teacher education. *Harvard Educational Review, 56*, 442–456.

Brownell, M. T., Ross, D. R., Colon, E. P., & McCallum, C. L. (2003). *Critical features of special education teacher preparation: A comparison with exemplary practices in general teacher education: Executive summary.* Gainesville, FL: Center on Personnel Studies in Special Education.

Calderhead, J. (1996). Teachers: Beliefs and knowledge. In D. C. Berliner & R. C. Calfee (Eds.), *Handbook of educational psychology* (pp. 709–725). New York: Macmillan.

Cochran-Smith, M. (2000, April). *The outcomes question in teacher education.* AERA Vice Presidential Address for Division K presented at the annual meeting of the American Educational Research Association, New Orleans, LA.

Connelly, E. M., & Clandinin, D. J. (1988). *Teachers as curriculum planners.* New York: Teachers College Press.

Council for Exceptional Children. (2003). *What every special educator must know: Ethics, standards, and guidelines for special educators* (5th ed.). Arlington, VA: Author.

Gitlin, A. (1990). Educative research, voice, and school change. *Harvard Educational Review, 60*, 443–466.

Greenwood, C. R. (2001). Introduction to topical issue: Bridging the gap between research and practice in special education. *Teacher Education and Special Education, 24*, 273–276.

Individuals with Disabilities Education Act (IDEA) Amendments of 1997, Pub. L. No. 105–117, 20 U.S.C. § 1400 *et seq.*

Johnson, L. J. (1996). Evolving transitions. *Teacher Education and Special Education, 19*, 202–205.

Johnson, L. J. (2002). *Testimony: U.S. House of Representatives Committee on Appropriations Subcommittee on Labor, Health and Human Services, Education, and Related Agencies.* Washington, DC: Author.

McKeon, R. (1952). Philosophy and action. *Ethics, 62*, 79–100.

National Center for Alternative Certification. (2004). *Alternative routes to teacher education: An overview.* Retrieved December 8, 2004, from http://www.teach-now.org/frmOverviewOfATC1.asp

Ohio Partnership for Accountability. (2003). *The impact of teacher education.* Columbus: Ohio Department of Education.

Otis-Wilborn, A., & Winn, J. (2000) The process and impact of standards-based teacher education reform. *Teacher Education and Special Education, 23*, 71–78.

Patton, J. M., Williams, B. T., Floyd, L. O., & Cobb, T. R. (2003). Recruiting and retaining culturally and linguistically diverse teachers in special education: Models for successful personnel preparation. *Teacher Education and Special Education, 26*, 288–303.

Rosenburg, M. S. (1996). Current issues facing teacher education and special education. *Teacher Education and Special Education, 19*, 209–211.

Sindelar, P. T., & Brownell, M. (2001). Research to practice dissemination, scale, and context: We can do it, but can we afford it? *Teacher Education and Special Education, 24,* 348–355.

Spooner, F., & Johnson, L. J. (1996). To stay the course or change: Reflections on preparing personnel in special education. *Teacher Education and Special Education, 19,* 202–205.

The Teaching Commission. (2004). *Teaching at risk: A call to action.* Washington, DC: Author. Retrieved May 2, 2004, from http://www.theteachingcommission.org/publications/FINAL_Report.pdf

U.S. Department of Education, National Center for Education Statistics. (2000). *Reference and reporting guide for preparing state and institutional reports on the quality of teacher preparation: Title II, Higher Education Act* (Rep. No. NCES 2000–089). Washington, DC: Author.

U.S. Department of Education, Office of Special Education and Rehabilitative Services. (2002). *A new era: Revitalizing special education for children and their families.* Washington, DC: Author.